New Darwinian Laws
Every Business Should Know

Related books

The Dark Matter and Dark Energy of Lean Thinking
The People Side of Lean Thinking
The HST Change Model
Transparent Management
Earn Their Loyalty
Mistake-Proofing Leadership

New Darwinian Laws
Every Business Should Know

Patrick Edmonds   Robert Brown

bp books

© 2016 Patrick Edmonds and Robert Brown

All Rights Reserved
Requests for permission to use or reproduce material from this book should be directed to books@collwisdom.com

Published by bp books
11700 Mukilteo Speedway #201-1084
Mukilteo WA 98275
USA

Cover Design by Elm Street Design Studio

Printed in the United States of America
by CreateSpace

Library of Congress Control Number: 2015938035

ISBN-13: 978-1502781956
ISBN-10: 1502781956

To Shannon: My wife and best friend. (Pat)

To Caitlin, Connor, Reagan and perhaps one or two grandchildren to be named later. You bring delight and adventure into my world. (Bob)

It is not the strongest or the most intelligent who will survive but those who can best manage change.
-Charles Darwin

I | Business: Nasty, Brutish, and Usually Short

In 2003, the Japanese construction company Kongo Gumi, Co. Ltd. celebrated 1,425 years in business. Created in 578 CE, the family-owned independent company traced its founding to Shitenno-ji, a Korean engineer brought to Japan to help build the Buddhist temple who stayed to create his own business. Sons, daughters, and sons-in-law ran the operation for centuries. Over its long history, this company built many famous buildings, one of which was the sixteenth century Osaka Castle. In the early 2000s it employed over one hundred people and enjoyed annual revenues of seventy million dollars. Alas, in 2006, like all individuals and eventually all companies, this ancient one succumbed, taken over by Takamatsu, a larger construction firm. The company had expanded its niche into buying land, borrowed money to do so, ran into a declining market, and could no longer service its loans: death from an inability to adapt to a changing environment.

It isn't a stretch to think of the business world as acting like the natural one. Mistakes can be deadly. Even doing the right thing doesn't guarantee survival. A good product, like film developed in a camera, can enjoy a brief time in the sun and then vanish. The world of Darwin is tough: short on sentiment and long on punishing weakness. There are no promises made, only the relentless pressure to adapt. Adapt and you live another day. Fail to adapt and you're gone.

Survival of the fittest is a fact, not a theory. Lessons proven over millions of years are available to help your business survive and thrive. All businesses, strong or weak, new or established, large or small, exist in an environment trying to destroy it. Competition is the most obvious threat. Changing demands and expectations of customers is another. A third are the selfish demands and the personal and collective flaws of the people who make up your organization.

Before any business existed and eons before *Homo sapiens* were a twinkle in anyone's eye, nature was honing a course all living things automatically followed. This process, evolution, tested the ability of organisms to adapt to changes in the environment. Those that adapted best survived. Those that didn't died out (over ninety-nine percent of all species who ever lived are now extinct). What happened then and continues to happen now is simple: adjust when you need to or you're gone.

To give you a solid basis for understanding how business can prosper from the wisdom of evolution, let's take a look at the dynamics of the process.

In the mid-nineteenth century, Charles Darwin spent five years on HMS *Beagle*. Onboard the *Beagle*, he examined specimens and formulated his theory that living things descended from one common ancestor. He was writing up his theory in 1858 when Alfred Russel Wallace sent him an essay describing the same idea. Darwin rushed his thinking into print and has the honor of being the one who brought to the masses the discomforting notion that we are the children of monkeys. Today, Darwin is so famous he's an adjective, while poor Wallace is a forgotten victim of the same evolutionary principle he espoused.

Life as we know it sprang from its simplest form around four billion years ago. Since then, natural changes in individual organisms passed to future generations, making it easier or harder for each species to survive. A favorable variation meant a species could adapt to a change in the environment, better compete in a stable environment, or move to and adapt to a different environment. Any of these positive events increased the chance of survival.

Other modifications, not so fortuitous, meant the organism would struggle to reach adulthood and procreate, and its offspring would also suffer a reduced chance of survival.

The evolutionary system operates because:

1. More offspring are born than can survive (think business *start-ups*)
2. Changes occur in individuals that can increase or decrease chances of survival (business decisions)
3. These changes are inheritable (business culture)

Darwin noted that when too many competed for limited resources, a struggle for existence ensued in which favorable changes enabled some to survive. This explains the diversity of living things as environmental and species changes occurred over long periods of time. Darwin's concept of natural selection describes how nature responds, for good or for ill, to individuals within species. He noted how artificial selection, consciously breeding the finest stock, also enhances the chances of survival or other preferred outcomes like size, nutritional needs, or resistance to disease.

Natural selection is a long, random process, like a river winding its way to the sea. There is no assessment of the situation, only random events, and no planned outcome, only what eventually happens. An individual animal lives or dies—it doesn't matter; the river makes it to the sea or becomes a lake; the outcome has no inherent value.

There are a few obvious realities to evolution. It functions because there are sufficient genetic variations in the population. Species that thrive in one environment niche are doomed if conditions change and they have no means to adapt. Buggy whip manufacturers come to mind.

Evolution isn't at the organism level, but at the level of genes, which have no interest in the outside world. Species survive or don't due to genetic changes that have nothing to do with responding to the environment. Species survival is an accident. Evolution is not smart; it does not have to be. Evolution just is. Your business, however, has to be smart and decide if the environment demands change or staying the course, as well as be able to make necessary and speedy changes.

Evolution works if traits that add to success are transmitted to progeny. Without this, subsequent generations lose evolutionary advantages. Traits that decrease survival chances should not be passed down. Companies that neglect their values and differentiating competencies often flounder in a sea of uncertainty and confusion.

Another obvious reality is fitness: the ability to survive and reproduce. Evolution (and survival) stops when either of these elements is missing. Offspring have to be both plentiful and have the right traits to overcome ubiquitous threats. Businesses will survive that adjust to changing market conditions and continue to produce products people want.

As we humans consider ourselves the top of the evolutionary ladder, we must pause at another evolutionary reality: simple organisms are the best adapted, and by an overwhelming margin. Most species are microscopic prokaryotes, forming half of the world's biomass. Complex life forms are just more noticeable, not better or higher—a lesson we will explore.

Another reality is adaptations work only if they provide advantages to a species. Adaptations are changes that enable an organism to be successful in its natural environment or to a changing environment. In nature, these adaptations are accidents of genetic change. For business purposes, adaptations must be thoughtful and the right ones—think artificial selection versus natural selection, and think good hiring and nurturing versus poor hiring and neglect.

Lastly, no two species can occupy the same niche for an extended period. Natural selection forces species to compete and to change. This change can be to adapt to the environment better than the competitor or to become better suited to a different environment. Sometimes it is necessary to give up one environment to thrive in another.

Although there is a kind of wisdom in natural selection, at least for surviving species, there is no value. The winning species is the one most suitable to the current environment. That species could vanish instantly, and the world would continue without remorse or regret. The same is true of the world of business; eventually people get over loss and memories fade over succeeding generations.

There is an opposing point of view that should be mentioned: intelligent design. Supporters of this view dismiss Darwin, evolution, and natural selection as a theory. They focus on a minor definition of theory as a yet unproven hypothesis. This approach declares life is irreducibly complex and anything that complex cannot have evolved, over no matter how many millennia. Their main thrust is along the lines of: if an eye lens is useless without a retina and a retina is useless without a lens, how could either have evolved first? They say only an intelligent entity, a God, could have created the complexities we see around us. We believe in intelligent design, at least in the context of the marketplace. Design your business the best you can; we're here to help.

How is evolution and Darwin's findings part of your business? To start, your business is run by someone whose cousins are apes and chimpanzees, with all the baggage that implies. It occupies no special place in the universe. Your business is in a constant struggle for survival. One day, your business will die. Our new Darwinian laws are culled from the effect of evolution, and the process. The outcome of natural selection is an organism that is most capable of competing for limited resources—a desirable state for your business.

Quality pioneer W. Edwards Deming declared, "Every system is perfectly designed to get the results it produces." Evolution produces organisms that are best adapted for the current environment. That's all it does. It does not produce the strongest or the fastest or the biggest, just the ones that are the most suitable. What this means for business is those that are the greatest fit with changing customer demand are most likely to survive and flourish. A business has neither the time nor the luxury of hoping the forces of evolution will help it to succeed. You must create a business that is a good fit for a fickle audience and one that creates compelling value for customers with increasing efficiency.

We will explore natural selection to learn what "fittest" means for businesses so we are not victims of unfortunate mutations, bad luck, or divine cruelty. We will also explore how social evolution can be a factor. Social evolution enables those not the fittest to survive through social support. For example, ill newborns who would die without intervention can often be saved, sometimes to live out full and rich lives, and other times to be burdened with lifelong ills.

The same is true for a business. It can contain untold deficits, but continue surviving through government intervention, adroit mergers, IPOs, and other infusions of life support.

We will explore how leaders make the mistake of acting as if what succeeded last year should work this year—or worse, what worked for the last fifty years will work for the next fifty. We will explore how little organizational structure has changed in the last ten thousand years and how this hinders company survival in today's rapidly changing environment.

Our goal is for you to manage a company that will be adaptable to change. In part, this means leadership is willing to listen and willing to hear the truth. It also means the entire company's response is quick, decisive, and effective, in unison, as demands change. It can mean the company alters the environment, creating changes itself that improve survivability.

Mother Nature is ruthless and uncaring. You must be ruthless too, but you don't have to be uncaring. In fact, if you understand that evolution works at the genetic level, and conceptualize that employees are like the genetic matter of an organization, you will value your people, the benefits of diversity, and the power of inclusion.

Natural selection has taught us that the key to survival is to adapt and adapt and adapt and adapt and adapt and adapt and adapt and adapt and…

New Darwinian laws can improve your chances of business survival and success. This book will help you understand what to adapt to and how. May you adapt well and thrive for a thousand years.

Table of Contents

1	Law of Connectedness *Small and Organized Beats Big, Strong, and Smart*	1
2	Law of Living Things *Natural Human Tendencies Can Kill (Your Business)*	19
3	Law of Design *Form Must Always Follow Function*	41
4	Law of Attraction and Neglect *What You Don't See Can Kill You*	69
5	Law of the Living Dead *Zombie Companies Create Zombie Workers*	87
6	Law of Malignancies *Internal Competition Causes Cancer*	107
7	Law of Good Health *Cooperation Cures Cancer*	135

8	Law of Boundaries *Amoebas Rule*	147
9	Law of Symbiosis *Survival Makes for Strange Bedfellows*	171
10	Law of Information *Information: Precious as Water*	185
	Conclusion	195
	Notes, Quotes, Do's and Don'ts	199
	About the Authors	215

Law of Connectedness

It is only when you watch the dense mass of
thousands of ants, crowded together around the hill,
blackening the ground, that you begin to see the
whole beast, and now you observe it thinking,
planning, calculating.
It is an intelligence, a kind of live computer,
with crawling bits for its wits.
-Lewis Thomas

1 | *Small and Organized Beats Big, Strong, and Smart*

Humans can't hold a candle to the collaboration of many of the most primitive creatures on the planet. In fact, numerous basic species have evolved into models of organizational behavior with such harmonization that they seem to be a single organism.

Organic cooperation is as helpful to the longevity of businesses as it is in nature. Organic cooperation describes individuals that act in such seamless collaboration that from the outside they appear to be a single and homogeneous entity, sometimes called superorganisms.

> When many work together for a goal, great things may be accomplished. It is said a lion cub was killed by a single colony of ants. - Sakya Pandita

Ants are an obvious example of superorganisms that have survived for a hundred and thirty million years. While ants can thrive as individual creatures, their ability to coalesce into a superorganism-like colony enables them to survive and thrive when food is scarce. Even individual humans can be thought of as superorganisms when we consider that a typical human digestive system contains 10^{13} to 10^{14} microorganisms.

Superorganisms

A superorganism's life force is to improve and survive at a much higher level than can be achieved by individuals. The advantages of the superorganism are obvious: the individual ant, bee, or bacterial cell is by itself small and often powerless in a world of much stronger predators. When associated with others who share a common survival interest, however, these unremarkable individuals can achieve extraordinary feats that far exceed the additive capability of each separate entity. The same is true in our own bodies. The human body is under constant attack by innumerable pathogens, and we're often unaware that this biological war rages around us due to our "superorganism" immunity responsiveness.

Superorganisms often evolve and learn through adaptive and even sophisticated collective knowledge sharing. Though unintelligent by themselves, creatures that participate in natural superorganisms rapidly share information and make decisions in ways that approximate how the human brain processes data. Research into the instinctive behavior bees use to dance and interact with other dancing bees shows a striking parallel to how primate neural networks process information to decide among competing alternatives. In fact, the cooperative behavior of bee and ant colonies is studied as a model for designing artificial neural networks to solve a wide range of optimization problems. This is true synergy—not the term whose meaning eludes each of us and has become an empty business cliché. This is a real force multiplier practiced to perfection each day by the unlikeliest of small creatures.

Coalescing into a superorganism is automatic for some lower life forms, but more difficult for us higher types.

Fortunately, research into biological superorganisms provides a workable blueprint for creating a *business* superorganism, which comprises six requirements.

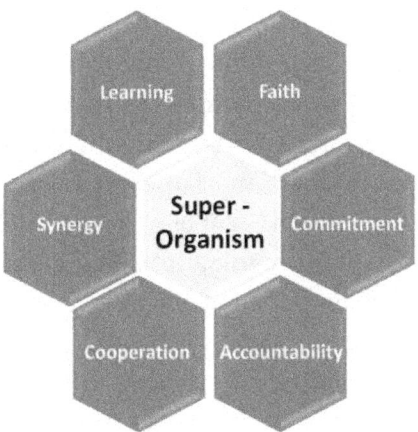

1. *Faith:* Participants must believe that joining the superorganism will lead to a better personal outcome than would otherwise be achieved in isolation, or else they won't join. This faith requires an implicit trust in and belief in one's fellow participants in the superorganism to do the right thing and do it well.

Participation in superorganisms is risky, because it poses a classic moral-hazard dilemma. Participants have to rely on the competence and integrity of their fellow members to achieve a better outcome than they would realize by optimizing for their own self-interest. This works fine when all members advance the needs of the organization first, but will unwind at the first suggestion of selfish intent.

2. *Commitment:* Successful superorganisms require that participants share an absolute commitment to the well-being of the greater organization. Members must subvert their own individual interests, and even their own identity, to the

greater good. Commitment at this level requires participants to share their talents and try their hardest because it's the right thing to do, not because it's asked or because they are being monitored.

3. *Accountability:* Each contributor in a superorganism is fallible and limited to its own individual potential. Because we are far from perfect despite our hopes and finest intentions, participants in superorganisms must hold themselves and each other accountable to their responsibilities in the organization. The greater interests of the organization are the driving concern. Energy and resources are routed straight to the area in greatest need to support the community's goals. Each participant is obligated to assist others when they need it, just as ants or bees will support one another if attacked.

4. *Cooperation:* Cooperation is a skill, and participation in a superorganism requires an extraordinary level of collaboration and teamwork far exceeding what some people can achieve. Desire alone to join a superorganism is insufficient. Not all people can cooperate, even if they want to. It's important for human superorganisms to screen candidates to make sure they have the potential and aspiration to be contributing, selfless members of the community. This also means that members who can't or won't cooperate with others are ejected.

5. *Learning:* A major advantage of superorganisms is their ability to evolve rapidly and make sound decisions through efficient information sharing. Superorganisms are learning organizations in which information is shared quickly and seamlessly to drive to optimal outcomes. In the process they learn how to realize even greater outcomes. Information is the lifeblood of twenty-first century business. Knowledge

flows unimpeded through a superorganism just as electrical impulses flow through a brain's neural network—decisions are rapid, and action is immediate. Human superorganisms cut out political pretense and protocols.

6. *Synergy:* While perhaps not a prerequisite for a superorganism, the most successful superorganisms invest in promoting a synergistic partnership with the world around them. Bees, for example, create honey and pollinate flowers, which increases their value to other animals and plants alike. Ant colonies play an important role by enhancing the decay of rotting vegetation and animals. Successful superorganisms make the world a better place even as they advance their own interests. In the same way, human superorganisms expand their value—and their probability of survival—by providing clear value to their community. Good citizenship can pay.

In nature, creatures like ants, bees, and amoebas organize into superorganisms because their DNA has programmed them to follow the six rules outlined above. In human organizations, we can understand and conform to the six rules of superorganisms if we so choose. The tricky part is that a superorganism culture requires every member to be willing to place the organization's needs above his or her own.

Vox Populi: The Raw Stuff of Human Superorganisms

Contestants in the popular television game show *Who Wants to be a Millionaire?* were asked progressively more difficult multiple-choice questions, each worth more prize money than the last. As they answered questions correctly, they earned the opportunity to stop and take the money or put their earnings on the line to answer a harder question. The stakes increased up to a one million dollar grand prize. Contestants owned three "lifelines" that they could exercise to help them if they got stuck: cut the multiple-choice options to two, phone a friend, or ask the audience. Interestingly, when the contestant invoked the audience lifeline, the answer was correct an astonishing ninety-four percent of the time! The audience consisted of average people, not a panel of experts.

The name for this dynamic, in which the aggregate answer provided by a large group is more likely to be correct than the answer provided by an individual, is the "wisdom of crowds." The wisdom of crowds idea suggests that, at least from an intelligence and decision-making perspective, humans have the innate capacity to collectivize into a kind of intellectual superorganism.

In his book *The Wisdom of Crowds*, James Surowiecki suggests that the following four key conditions separate so-called wise crowds from irrational crowds:

- *Diversity of opinion*: Each person should have their own unique understanding even if it's just an eccentric interpretation of established facts
- *Independence*: People's opinions aren't subject to the opinions of those around them
- *Decentralization*: People can specialize and draw on their own private knowledge base
- *Aggregation*: Some mechanism exists for turning individual assessments into a collective decision

When all four criteria are in effect, a group can achieve a better answer than would otherwise be reached by an individual. Research suggests that the greater the diversity of the group, the more likely collective decision-making will be correct. In effect, the wisdom of crowds principle can have the potential to help shape a smart human superorganism.

If we have this innate ability to approximate the collective intelligence advantage of the superorganism, why do most organizations fail to realize the benefit? Why do we suppress the voice of most of our employees? Why do we invest significant decision-making authority in a single person or small cadre of leaders instead? There are two common excuses, one a cop-out and the other a cruel vestige of a Charles Dickens-style worldview. The cop-out is that it is too hard and takes too much time for us to coordinate our thoughts at a superorganism level in our organizations. The cruel lie is that most employees lack enough intellectual value to warrant being asked their opinions. To that we say if primitive creatures like ants, bees, and amoebas can cooperate and communicate so well, people should have no excuse not to coalesce into superorganisms.

We Get In Our Own Way

The brain of each animal is hardwired with a limited ability to change. The more primitive the creature, the harder it is for individuals to change. Conversely, the higher the level of the organism, the faster it can learn and therefore change. DNA drives the societies of many less sophisticated creatures to cooperate and communicate well through instinct. Human organizations are entangled with the self-inflicted complexity of personality conflicts, vanity-fueled ambition, well-intended but misguided policies, and mistrust. Each day, we tie ourselves up in more knots, making it that much harder to work together and to share ideas. Imagine an organization in which each person's thoughts could connect with the minds of the right people who could share the idea, immediately and unfiltered. This would be like connecting the synapses of multiple people. While technology like email, mobile phones, and Instant Messenger can help to promote the exchange of ideas, they can also be our bane. Just look at the truckloads of messages that pile up in most inboxes and voice mail boxes each day.

Is it possible for people to join into a superorganism, or are we too smart for our own good? We invent tools and techniques that seem to make our lives more complex. Maybe our technology has already taken over.

W. L. Gore & Associates: A Case Study In Human Superorganisms

In 1958, chemist Bill Gore and his wife Vieve started a small company in their home to make insulated electronic ribbon cables. Over time, Gore grew his company, W. L. Gore & Associates, into an international corporation with a diverse product portfolio that now includes medical applications, guitar strings, and its famous waterproof Gore-Tex fabric.

Today, W. L. Gore & Associates is one of the two hundred largest private companies in the United States, with 2010 revenues of two and a half billion dollars. The corporation employs around nine thousand associates at over fifty facilities throughout the world.

In 2012, *Fortune* magazine recognized W. L. Gore & Associate on its "Best Companies to Work For" list in the US for the fifteenth consecutive year. Its subsidiaries have won similar acclaim in the UK, Germany, Italy, France, and Sweden.

What accounts for the company's enviable and sustained record of achievement? For fifty years, the corporation has evolved into a most unusual—and to its employees, exceptional—culture. Bill Gore designed the company's culture to encourage and empower employees to innovate, to advance the organization by tapping into their potential.

The Gore culture is based on the concept of a lattice organization. This is an egalitarian organization with few job titles, in which employees evaluate one another's performance and each employee is a shareholder after one year. The company's website describes the concept:

> Gore's unique "lattice" management structure, which illustrates a nonhierarchical system based on interconnection among associates, is free from traditional bosses and managers. There is no assigned authority, and we become leaders based on our ability to gain the respect of our peers and to attract followers.
>
> You will be responsible for managing your own workload and will be accountable to others on your team. More importantly, only you can make a commitment to do something (for example, a task, a project, or a new role)—but once you make a commitment, you will be expected to meet it.

The culture is based on four Fundamental Beliefs and four Guiding Principles, which are more than the usual corporate talking points. This is what they say.

Fundamental Beliefs:

- *Long-Term View:* Our investment decisions are based on long-term payoff, and our Belief in the Individual: if you trust individuals and believe in them, they will be motivated to do what's right for the company.
- *Power of Small Teams:* Our lattice organization harnesses the fast decision-making, diverse perspectives, and collaboration of small teams.
- *All in the Same Boat:* All Gore associates are part owners of the company through the associate stock plan. Not only does this allow us to share in the risks and rewards of the company, it gives us an added incentive to stay committed to its long-term success. As a result, we feel we are all in this effort together, and believe we should always consider what's best for the company as a whole when making decisions.
- *Fundamental beliefs are not sacrificed for short-term gain.*

Guiding Principles:

- *Freedom:* The company was designed to be an organization in which associates can achieve their own goals best by directing their efforts toward the success of the corporation: action is prized, ideas are encouraged, and making mistakes is viewed as part of the creative process. We define freedom as being empowered to encourage each other to grow in knowledge, skill, scope of responsibility, and range of activities. We believe that associates

will exceed expectations when given the freedom to do so.
- *Fairness:* Everyone at Gore sincerely tries to be fair with each other, our suppliers, our customers, and anyone else with whom we do business.
- *Commitment:* We are not assigned tasks; rather, we each make our own commitments and keep them.
- *Waterline:* Everyone at Gore consults with other associates before taking actions that might be "below the waterline"—causing serious damage to the company.

An enduring aspect of the Gore culture is the notion of dabble time. Gore associates are granted about ten percent of their workweek to apply to developing new ideas, and prototyping is encouraged. When an employee wants to be a product champion, she must convince others to dedicate their dabble time to the endeavor. In this way, promising ideas are tested and supported through the faith and grassroots energy of colleagues. Those who can persuade others to follow their lead become leaders in the company.

Synaptic Communication

Members of a superorganism share impulses without having to pass through intermediaries. Lattice organizations enable workers to share ideas without the delays of unnecessary approvals or the queue time incurred by crossing organizational silos. In this way, lattice companies allow the organizational approximation of the direct exchange of neural information across our synapses—synaptic communication.

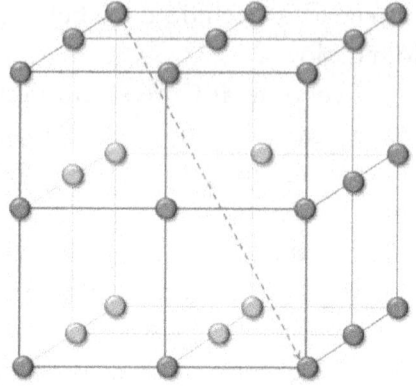

Members in the lattice are encouraged to explore novel ideas and are trusted to do the right thing. Due to the egalitarian nature of the lattice structure, members form teams to develop their own plans and collaborate to achieve team goals. Rather than having to navigate non-value-added communication channels, workers are expected to communicate directly with others whom they believe can be of immediate help.

In a lattice structure, influence and credibility are gained through contribution, innovation, and skill, as opposed to positional authority and titles. Some individuals in a lattice cannot convince others to support their ideas. Those employees will either have to reposition themselves and their ideas to be of more value to the organization, or leave. There is an elegant dynamic of self-policing that occurs in an environment in which each member must be accountable to provide value to the organization. Unproductive overhead is largely alien in such a model.

Survival Guide

Organizations that are as collaborative and effective as W. L. Gore & Associates are rare. As companies grow, it becomes more challenging to work together. It's ironic that, despite our larger brains and capacity for learning, we are no match for the humble ants and bees. We paralyze ourselves through our own bureaucracy rather than focus our efforts on driving more internal cooperation.

To understand how close your organization is to being a superorganism, consider the following checklist. Mark the appropriate box for each category, and tally up the marks for each category at the end.

R = Never/Rarely S = Sometimes A = Often/Always

	R	S	A
Faith			
Employees are confident that the organization has their best interest in mind.	—	—	—
Employees have confidence that their managers can be trusted to do a great job.	—	—	—
Managers do not feel the need to micromanage.	—	—	—
Faith – TOTAL	—	—	—

Commitment

Employees understand the organization's vision and are committed to its success.   __ __ __

Employees are intrinsically motivated to put forth their best efforts.   __ __ __

Managers trust that employees are intrinsically committed to the success of the organization.   __ __ __

Commitment – TOTAL   __ __ __

Accountability

Employees hold themselves and their peers accountable to fulfill their responsibilities.   __ __ __

Employees willingly and immediately assist others on their team when needed.   __ __ __

Employees willingly and immediately assist others on another team when needed.   __ __ __

Accountability – TOTAL   __ __ __

Cooperation

Candidates for new roles are evaluated for ability to collaborate and desire to work in teams.   __ __ __

Employees seek opportunities to work in teams.   __ __ __

The most innovative or high impact outputs are created by teams rather than individuals working alone.   __ __ __

Employees who cannot or will not collaborate are removed. — — —

Cooperation – TOTAL — — —

Learning

Effective communication skills within and across teams are a core strength of the organization. — — —

When errors are identified and corrected, the corrective information is shared across the organization to prevent its recurrence. — — —

Information is not viewed as a basis of organizational power that should be hoarded. — — —

Learning – TOTAL — — —

Synergy

The organization invests in improving its community. — — —

The communities in which the organization operates appreciate that the organization is there. — — —

Synergy – TOTAL — — —

If your organization scored fewer Often/Always than Sometimes or Never/Rarely in one or more categories, then there is work to be done to become a superorganism.

If your organization scored fewer Often/Always than Sometimes or Never/Rarely across every category, you have a solid foundation to become a superorganism. Your efforts should be to hone these capabilities into a solid framework of success.

Law of Living Things

Was man, indeed, at once so powerful, so virtuous and magnificent, yet so vicious and base? He appeared at one time a mere scion of the evil principle, and at another as all that can be conceived of noble and godlike. To be a great and virtuous man appeared the highest honour that can befall a sensitive being; to be base and vicious, as many on record have been, appeared the lowest degradation, a condition more abject than that of the blind mole or harmless worm. For a long time I could not conceive how one man could go forth to murder his fellow, or even why there were laws and governments; but when I heard details of vice and bloodshed, my wonder ceased, and I turned away with disgust and loathing.
-Mary Shelley, *Frankenstein*

2 | Natural Human Tendencies Can Kill (Your Business)

Slavery can be traced to the earliest human records, back even before the Code of Hammurabi c. 1760 BCE. It existed in Egypt during the time of the pharaohs. It existed during the time of the Crusades in the Middle Ages. And it exists today. In 1117, Iceland was the first European country to outlaw slavery. In 1981, Mauritania was the last country to abolish slavery. In spite of this long history of abolition, it is estimated that between twelve and twenty-seven million people live as slaves today, many of them in Mauritania.

As bad as it sounds, things have been worse. David Forsythe noted, "...at the beginning of the Nineteenth Century an estimated three-quarters of all people alive were trapped in bondage against their will either in some form of slavery or serfdom."

Pre-Industrial Revolution, the average workday was between eleven and fourteen hours, or more. The length of the workday depended on the length of daylight. Once machines came into use, it was common to light a candle or two in a dank stone building and subject workers to twelve- to sixteen-hour days. Since farms still had to be tended, children supplied much of this machine labor. In Britain of the late 1700s, for example, about two-thirds of the labor force in the textile industry were children.

Even nineteenth century reform did little to improve the average worker's lot. For example, England's first Factory Act in 1802 provided meager protection, such as limiting the work hours of children to twelve hours per day. While most industrialists ignored the law, this early effort raised awareness and smoothed the way for later factory acts.

Life improved in 1833 in England with the first law limiting work hours. Regulations limited miners to twelve hours and children to eight hours per day. More joy was felt throughout the land in 1848 when the government enacted a ten-hour day. The Factory and Workshop Act of 1901 and subsequent English laws continued to improve the lot of children and other workers, including raising the minimum working age to twelve and addressing education, meals, and fire escapes. These English laws and the many others enacted around the world were necessary because of the inequality between employer and worker. Before these laws, and when central governments were weak, life was even worse. Thomas Hobbes famously described reality in his *Leviathan*, published in 1651. His view was similar to the dog-eat-dog world of business:

> ...In such condition, there is no place for Industry...no Knowledge of the face of the Earth; no account of Time; no Arts; no Letters; no Society; and which is worst of all, continuall feare, and danger of violent death; And the life of man, solitary, poore, nasty, brutish, and short.

In contrast, starting in 1914, Henry Ford paid his assembly workers the unheard-of sum of five dollars a day. He also reduced daily work hours from nine to eight. This stroke of genius motivated workers to travel from all over for these jobs, and it enticed them to remain at their mind-numbing work. Ford also enabled this emerging middle class to afford the cars that were now racing off assembly lines.

Today, for the average Joe and his family, life is a two-car garage, home-delivered pizza, and a few hours on the couch in front of the plasma flat-screen. Despite our economic woes, the average worker is far better off than in any time in history. That's the good news.

The bad news is disappointing. Twenty years ago, according to the Conference Board's consumer research, sixty-one percent of workers expressed satisfaction with their jobs. Today, that percentage is less than half. Gallup and others have determined that a mere twenty-seven percent of employees are emotionally engaged in their work. The rest are disengaged or actively disengaged, actually acting out their unhappiness. The Gallup people further estimate that this dissatisfaction costs employers $350 billion in lost productivity.

The source of all these issues, problems and despair is called the "Organization-Individual Divide (O-I)" (*Transparent Management*, Robert Brown, bp books). There is always a gap between organizational needs, values, and goals and those of the individuals who work at that organization. The tension occurs when the perceived needs of the business conflict with the needs of the employees. The gap was insurmountable between slave owner and slave to the point of management control over every element of life and death.

For Mom and Pop businesses, the gap can be reversed, sacrificing the good of the company for the happiness of the spouse or family members. The gap often fluctuates with the various business decisions that are made, the different needs of organizations and expectations of employees, personal relationships, variation in the general economy, and other day-to-day and month-to-month realities of life. As simple as this O-I Divide idea is, many managers seem oblivious to its existence.

The Story of Steve

Steve is a service quality specialist in a hospital complaint department. He works with five others who respond to phone, letter, email, and walk-in complaints. In an eight-hour day, he handles up to twenty complaints of varying complexity. His boss, Martha, spends time in the office with the other workers, but most often attends department meetings and provides customer service training and manager coaching where needed.

Because Steve is good at his job and has been doing it for three years, Martha doesn't worry about his performance. She can check the computer data to monitor his work: how many complaints, how many resolved and pending, and how he compares to the other employees. The data show Steve is performing above standard.

The data, however, do not show that Steve is more and more dissatisfied with his job. He feels stuck. A management position somewhere would be more to his liking. Each day brings less satisfaction and more frustration. Steve continues to do his job, but the gap between him and the company is widening. Although Martha stops and chats with her staff and holds regular meetings, she never bothers to ask the right questions to encourage Steve to share his current dissatisfaction. She is surprised when he puts in his two-week notice to leave the hospital to join an investment company as a trainee, even though the new position pays less.

Bosses

This scenario must occur thousands of times a day. A Gallup poll determined that the number one reason people leave a job is a poor relationship with the immediate supervisor. A poor relationship doesn't have to be acrimonious; perceived indifference by the boss is often enough.

Managers are interested in getting the work done, not babysitting during the workday, and not nodding with sympathy while listening to the woes of the weekend. No matter who comes through the door each day, and no matter what their emotional or physical state, managers feel pressured to get the work done. Managers believe they have to figure out how to organize a range of human beings to work together to do what must be done.

By convention, we are conditioned to think that without such organization—the manager as the metronome and employees keeping pace—businesses would fail. People are hired to play a position, like a football linebacker. The coach (manager) calls the play and everyone springs into action until the play is done and the game is won or lost. In reality, this metaphor doesn't hold up. Work rarely means winning anything of value. For employees, a good day at work often means you put in your time without being bothered by supervisors, and you go home on time.

Most workers are told what to do and how to do it, with little joy from the work except for the paycheck at the end of the pay period. That kind of rote behavior and that kind of postponed reward is the lot of most people who go to work for that paycheck, do a job they don't like much, and work for a boss who doesn't seem to care.

Many managers are either unaware of or unconcerned by the level of stress endured by their employees. Yet, stress causes half of the annual five hundred fifty million days of absence. Eighty percent of medical expenditures are stress-related. Overall, stress costs US companies between two hundred and three hundred billion dollars a year. Something is causing all this stress.

There is an optimal level of arousal for any task. Take cooking, for example. Fixing cold cereal requires little arousal. Microwaving soup requires just a little more. Baking brownies from a packaged mix requires some arousal, while preparing a massive Thanksgiving dinner might require the most. Our guess is that most managers do not understand the right amount of arousal needed to do the task. Do the work, don't make waves, get your paycheck, and be glad of it.

If you believe that people live in an emotional and physical world, that they experience physical and emotional pain, that people have needs and interests they cannot let go at the entryway, that workers are neither slaves nor children, then you must realize that employees are often treated like crap.

Workers are demeaned as "resources," "headcounts," or "FTEs" instead of people. They are treated as expendable, as expenses to be minimized. They are disrespected or ignored. We might not say it aloud, but our actions as managers suggest that we'll replace them with robots or cheap offshore labor at the first opportunity. We have laws to govern our behavior, but our managerial behavior can be unconscionable, even if legal. It is no wonder so few American employees feel emotional engagement in their work, that so many leave a good job because of a bad manager. It is clear to any knowledgeable observer that managers do not know how to manage.

Our experience and conclusion, and probably yours, is that most managers were at one time capable individual contributors who were promoted into management with little training and support. With newfound gravitas, some even don a suit when they used to come to work in real work clothes. But a suit does not a manager make. Many look good but have no clue how to do good.

Professor (and former pro football player) Herbert Blumer's theory of symbolic interactionism predicts the sad outcome of managerial ignorance. Blumer said we interact symbolically in three ways: meaning, language, and thought. A new supervisor who now wears a tie is conveying to his old buddies, "I am no longer one of you." He is saying, "I am different than before, more powerful, more important than you." He is now part of the Organization-Individual Divide and is declaring, "You will treat me differently, and I will treat you differently." New supervisor and old buddies now have a new meaning to their relationship, one of distance, power, and control. Their communication will change; once it was talking by the watercooler, now it will be email. And thoughts will change too; people will interpret behavior differently, and words will become laden with innuendo.

Although they wouldn't want to admit it, most managers treat employees like cogs-in-wheels, at least occasionally.

Even good managers can slip into destructive managerial behavior unintentionally. Are managers draconian? Is there a general flaw in their character? When someone becomes a manager, do they morph into a sadist? The answer to these questions is yes.

Studies have shown that for many human characteristics, from intelligence to customer service, most people classify themselves as above average. This is operationalizing pride. No one wants to be merely average (although some will say they are—not believing it for a second), so everyone feels above average; not much, but enough to fulfill the needs of dignity and self-esteem. Mistakes, those ever-present threats to dignity and self-esteem, must be avoided or minimized by all those living the above-average lie. Pity the poor manager who points out simple errors without the benefit of superhuman diplomacy.

People are not machines. It would be much easier to arrive at work and push a button to start an employee. Managers arrive at work and face the necessity of interaction with a mélange of human beings to get the work done. Managers are paid to make sure the work gets done using, and perhaps in spite of, his allotted labor. It is a misguided manager who doesn't realize that people are a part of the problem and the major resource for the solution.

It is our belief that the higher in the leadership hierarchy a manager climbs, the poorer manager they tend to become. The Peter Principle, which states that people advance to their level of incompetence, is alive and flourishing. A manager newly up the ranks from line staff is often undertrained and overstressed. As one climbs the corporate ladder, the tendency is to become distant from the work itself, and the people who do the work, in favor of strategy, faultfinding, appearances, and judgmental responses. The stakes increase the higher you go, and the now more distant lower ranks of people become more expendable too.

Managers are only a part of the reason so many employees have a pathetic work experience. We hinted at it earlier when we mentioned arousal levels. Too many workers experience a minimal sense of excitement, well-being, or accomplishment each day. How can they? Most do their jobs adequately, day after day, with little change week to week and year to year. Even the worst baseball player will occasionally get a hit and enjoy that run to first base. Few employees experience anything so rewarding. They spend most of their waking hours playing the role of an expendable cog with little sense that their effort makes a difference in the world. They go to work and come home. They go to work and come home. They go to work and come home. They get a paycheck every few weeks.

There is evidence that people who have a best friend at work stay in the job longer than those who don't. One conclusion from this finding is that people meet some of their emotional needs at work—when they can. Another research finding is that people on teams perform better than people who are not on teams. This suggests that human connections are important for performance.

One way undertrained managers try to create this connection is to interact with employees reflective of their age. You've heard that each generational segment—the Veterans, Baby Boomers, Generation X, Generation Y, and Millennials—has its own defining characteristics. The idea is that if you don't take these differences into account, you are not an effective leader. If you understand generational differences, the thinking goes, you're better able to create teams and inspire each type of worker. Some believe that each generation has its distinct set of behaviors, habits, attitudes, and interests. If you believe that by being born anywhere within a twenty-year span creates a classifiable personality, you either don't understand people or, maybe worse, you think putting people into such a box enables you to manage them better. A clue to the absurdity of this idea is to reflect on how the boundaries of each generation are defined. If it is based on a calendar date rather than an abrupt and measurable change in the personalities of the babies being born on either side of the boundary, it makes no sense.

Another box managers get trapped in is to confuse the concept of fairness with treating everyone the same. A fairness policy would require us to enforce consistent policies that do not infringe on the basic rights of workers; however, mandates to treat all workers with the same generic approach, no matter what their individual needs, are the norm. Often uniform treatment is a policy handed down from HR or Legal. It's easier, more HR-friendly, but is it the best way to run the show? No, it is not. People are not the same. How can anyone think that treating everyone the same makes sense? It makes sense only if you do not understand how to manage individuals, and you take the line of least resistance. No one can complain if you treat everybody alike. Mission accomplished. "We can't help it if someone has individual needs and is dissatisfied; here we promote 'fairness'—everyone is treated the same." It must be almost magical to work at this kind of place. The Stepford Tool and Die Company treats everyone the same. Heck, the entire town of Pleasantville treated everyone the same, and their high school basketball team won all of its games!

We know of a company that defined fair treatment of its receptionists as each of them being scheduled to open and close the office at least one time each week (except for the supervisor, who came up with the idea). This resulted in some people working late one night and coming in early the next morning. Fair also meant changing existing schedules whenever there was a new hire so each person had an equal chance at a good schedule. Is fair treating everyone the same or id fair rewarding employees proportionate to their contributions?

Finally, managers often fall into the trap of believing they don't have enough time to spend with employees to observe what is happening at the staff level. When not running from fire to fire, managers spend much of their time in meetings and processing emails. In our consulting work we see this dynamic play out in every industry and in organizations of every size. The root cause is almost always the same: failure to prioritize what's important, especially empowering the growth of employees who actually do the work. If managers prioritized the empowerment of employees to make more decisions and problem-solve, managers could have more time to focus on long-term issues instead of fighting day-to-day fires.

We have to do better. Most managers have no idea how to manage, because they are ill-suited to manage and receive inadequate training and support when it comes to learning how to manage well. They are poor managers because they are promoted into management positions they have no business taking. They receive abysmal training and support because the higher-level decision-makers also receive abysmal training and support—and, as we mentioned, have become too removed from the action.

People are living things and need what living things need, even at work.

Doing Better

What does it mean to "treat people as living things" at work? You may have some guesses. You may even believe that what you do now is the right way of growing your employees. Since you're interested enough to read this book, that's possible, but unlikely. We've seen few companies that do it even pretty well. We have seen no company do it as well as it can be and should be done. Most places stink.

Let's look at one critical concept: respect. Do you believe that respecting employees is an absolute necessity to treating them as living things? Most living things only require respect to the degree we don't harm them; they can handle most life demands on their own if we don't interfere. People are different. People, your employees, thrive on basic respect. They don't live on it, they don't need it to continue to show up in the morning, they don't even demand it, but without it, you and your organization incur a massive opportunity cost from lost production and lost potential.

What are you doing to show respect to your employees?

The respect litmus test is if the supervisor knows the employee's work, understands how the employee feels about it, appreciates the employee's efforts, and the employee knows that. That is respect.

Here's an example of a normal (and thus disrespectful) situation:

> Rachel is a newly minted salesperson for Dennison Chemicals. She is on the road twice the time her colleagues are and is tired of it. She mentions this to her boss. Her boss, unfortunately, is unprepared to be a boss (but was a terrific salesperson and therefore promoted to management). He replies that she is not on the road more than other new salespeople, and even if she were she would grow from the extra experience. Her boss continues with several reasons why the current situation is good for the company and good for Rachel's development. He asks no questions to further understand Rachel's point of view. Discouraged, Rachel relents (and takes another step away from full engagement with her firm).

What's missing is obvious: a dialogue between boss and employee about how the employee sees things. Most bosses tell; they must learn how to ask. As we suggested, most are focused on the work and the outcome, and not the human being doing the work. What a horrendous insult to the most important ally for a prosperous business. Her boss had no clue who Rachel was and what mattered to her. From his perspective, the conversation was a success. How sad.

But here's the dilemma: someone, the CEO, the founder, the board, some visionary, had the idea that there was an opportunity to make something better. All that was needed to turn the opportunity into reality was the right goal, a little hard work, and the commitment to overcome adversity on the way to success. The company hired a core of workers to fulfill that vision, and everything was ready. But no one told the workers. (Some startups are glorious exceptions—in these, everybody is pulling an oar in the same direction, toward an uncertain final port, but with pride and dedication; a benefit of having peers working together.) Workers are told what to do, monitored to make sure they're doing what they were told to do, and rewarded when they fit someone's idea of a job description. There are rules and regulations, job performance reviews, and quotas and guidelines, along with dozens of other administrative flotsam between the worker and the boss. Most managers do not understand how the work should be done or how to treat people as they should be treated. Some managers want to improve; they seek training and concepts to help them. Unfortunately, most of these efforts are one-size-fits-all solutions and that may only make the situation worse. As newly learned training fades over time, it is back to business as usual.

Grow

"Grow" means that people, in this case your employees, are being appropriately challenged, supported in their responses to these challenges, and successful in addressing difficult challenges. Grow also means that responding to challenges creates an increasing sense of confidence and well-being. Lastly, grow means the person reaches personal goals, enjoys greater self-esteem, and connects more positively with others. Does this happen at your company? Is support for growth part of how the company is designed? You may think so; many companies develop people by providing experiences that will stretch them. This is a good thing to do. Most times, however, this support is limited to a favored few, those destined to become leaders. The average Joe is stuck just doing his job.

The more such experiences and goals are promoted for all employees the better. This is especially true if the experiences and goals are equally weighted for the benefit of the company and the employee, and that everyone in the company knows this is happening.

Each employee must have the chance to grow. Otherwise, you have no right hiring them. We understand the economics of hiring low skill workers for low skill jobs, providing minimal training and being cavalier about how much turnover this system creates. It isn't cost-effective to do otherwise, so it seems. But maybe all the costs of such a practice aren't enumerated; maybe all the costs can't be enumerated. But there are costs. It is costly and distracts managers' time to recruit, hire onboard, and train. The bad reputation organizations incur for abusing staff can be even more damaging. Investing in the growth of employees is exactly that: an investment in the future of the organization, not a throwaway expense.

The Three Secrets

There are three simple secrets that will help managers to grow their people.

One: The first secret of growing employees is to make sure their boss knows how to listen to them, does listen to them, reflects on what is heard, and responds. That's it: listening and responding. No one has to take a Myers-Briggs assessment. You don't have to have team meetings. You don't have to hire expert consultants. To listen is a simple idea, yet difficult to do. We've mentioned all the administrative detritus that smothers true interpersonal connection. Bosses have an image to maintain among their peers and managers of not being soft. The Human Resources department has to keep order. The Legal department works to steer the company out of harm's way. There are rules to follow, images to maintain, roles to play.

"Play" is the right word. We play at being professional, serious, goal-oriented, controlled, impersonal, disciplined, etcetera—all the wrong things to make an organization hum with the music of people caring about each other and joining to get the work done. Professionalism might just be the worst idea anyone has come up with to create the finest environment for work.

Some of the best advice you can give to someone about how to relate to others is "just be yourself." There is no need for rehearsed lines, special clothes, props, or forced dialogue. Be yourself. This is our advice for managers who want to listen to their employees. If you care about the people who work with you, all you have to do is express that, and then listen. If you don't care about them, close this book, return it, and try to get your money back. Also consider a move to a place that endorses indentured servitude; that's where you might be a better fit.

When done right, the Toyota Production System (now called Lean Thinking in most places) puts emphasis on respecting people. A useful way show respect is to ask people their opinion and listen to what they have to say. And, as often as practical, act on what they tell you.

Two: The second secret to growing employees is creating "we." It's the boss and employees, working together to accomplish what is important to accomplish. The core of we is a sense of belonging. That's why young men with no other advantages join gangs. The risk of prison or death by drive-by shooting is preferable to being isolated and alienated. Businesses can create high-performing teams that are immensely rewarding, but few bother to do so.

Set team goals. There is no better way to rally a team than to focus on a common cause. Focus that sense of "we." Channel the team into waging a common effort to achieve positive and measurable goals.

Three: Get constant feedback. Without feedback (part of listening), you won't know how you're doing. Without feedback, you will have to operate from your own limited perceptions. There are many ways to create feedback.

Much of the power that Lean Thinking generates for effective change is via visual control. Observers can see what needs to be done and how it is being done. Workers should define standard work so even the newest employee knows what to do. Employees should be able to see and hold themselves and one another accountable for work being done according to plan.

Once a standard for the work is established, continuous improvements can be made. The same can be true for growing people if feedback is considered the verbal form of visual control. Compared to visual control, however, feedback is often destructive. Here is why. Visual control works well when actions are physical, where results can be seen directly. It may be easy to notice if a nut falls off a bolt and to identify the cause. With people, however, the action is often internal—a thought or a feeling drove the behavior. Feedback on the behavior alone is an affront to ego. Feedback should also be given for positive effort and/or outcomes. If feedback is also given for positive results, which occur far more often than negative, the occasional negative feedback can be more easily digested.

Feedback is the driver for growing the human beings you hired and promised to help grow. Sam Walton said it well:

"Outstanding leaders go out of their way to boost the self-esteem of their personnel. If people believe in themselves, it's amazing what they can accomplish."

Positive energy is needed for growth. The boss should be a source of that positive energy. A leader who believes in her workers can inspire them to grow. Recall your favorite high school teacher. That person probably provided the positive energy required for people growth. Be that way and you will do better than almost everyone else.

Survival Guide

How effective is your time spent as a manager? Complete the following chart of how you spend your time during a typical workweek. Identify between four and ten categories of how your time is spent, such as email processing, customer meetings, internal meetings, time training staff, etc. Even if your schedule varies week-to-week, it's okay to generalize how you spend your time.

Activity Category	% Time / Week	Employee-Facing (Y/N)?

Use the table to construct a pie chart of your typical week. If your employee-facing time is less than twenty-five percent, you should reexamine your priorities to see if there are opportunities to engage more with your team. If your employee-facing time is less than ten percent, you should come to terms with the fact you don't know what's going on with your team or how they feel. You are at risk of working in a filtered and detached bubble.

Law of Design

It is the pervading law of all things organic and inorganic, of all things physical and metaphysical, of all things human and all things super-human, of all true manifestations of the head, of the heart, of the soul, that the life is recognizable in its expression, that form ever follows function.
This is the law.
-Louis Sullivan, "The Tall Office Building Artistically Considered"

3 | *Form Must Always Follow Function*

If you asked a platypus if his or her appearance was odd or embarrassing, you'd surely get a quizzical look. If the platypus responded at all, it would say, "You must be joking. I am perfectly designed for what I want to do."

Form must follow function; however, conventional organizational design requires function to follow form. You need to fix that.

Hierarchical Pyramids Suck

If you asked one hundred random corporations to describe their organizational structure, ninety-nine would hand you a copy of a classic organization chart with one node at the top that branches through increasing numbers of boxes and rows as you proceed down the page. (Incidentally, the hundredth random company would have the same *de facto* model but would not be organized enough to find a copy of it). This prototypical organization design is a pyramid model, a structure that people (like many other social animals) have relied on to organize themselves from time immemorial.

The traditional pyramidal paradigm is a modern day version of feudalism. There is scarce room for a privileged few, the executives, to wield most of the power and resources.

This elite cadre must be served and their position protected by a somewhat larger tier of modern day petty nobles, now called middle managers. Middle managers are the insulation and direct interface between the executive tier and the workers who actually deliver value. Like petty nobles, the value of the middle manager is often suspect to executives and workers alike; they neither determine the strategic course of the organization, nor do they deliver any value directly to customers. Senior leaders may view middle managers as a necessary evil at best, and as overhead at worst. Workers often view them as enforcers and time wasters.

As a result, the survival of a middle manager usually combines (1) artful politicking, sacrificed work-life balance, and tolerance for personal degradation to secure adequate patronage and (2) self-promotion to appear more useful or capable than middle manager peers. Like a feudal hierarchy, the system must be supported by a large foundation of workers who generate the value but have little influence over or share the organization's resources. Workers are treated as fungible or expendable. Since there are decreasing opportunities for advancement at each tier in the hierarchy, the pyramid model requires periodic purges. Employees at any level whose potential is deemed to be maxed out at their current level may be marginalized or pushed out of the organization. In effect, workers are treated as consumable commodities to fuel an endless cycle of performance review-based culling.

It is not coincidental that a typical organizational design mirrors the classic energy pyramid, a simple graphical model to show how energy flows in a living ecosystem. Only the lowest and largest energy tier consists of producers, who provide energy to the system from external sources. Consumers, who devour members of lower tiers to obtain their energy, occupy each higher level in the food chain.

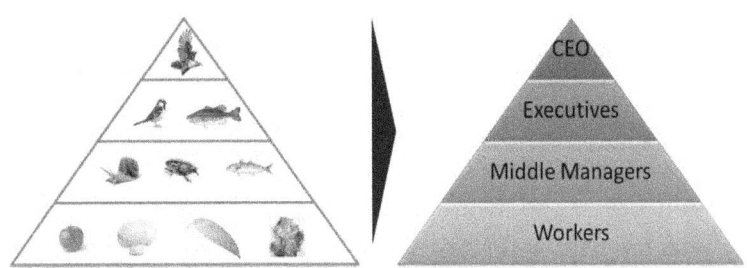

Two interesting parallels arise from the comparison of the energy pyramid with the classic organizational hierarchy.

First, only the bottom tier of each pyramid interacts outside of the system in a meaningful way. Just as plants convert solar energy into food sources to supply the rest of the food chain, those who produce for the entire organization are cast at the lowest levels of the hierarchy. With each higher tier in both pyramids, the participants are removed further and further from the original source of energy, which are customers in the organizational pyramid.

Second, the rule of thumb in energy pyramids is that only about ten percent of the energy is passed from one level to the next higher level. In the same way, in organizational pyramids, massive amounts of information and insight—about customers, competitors, and partners—fail to transcend each higher tier in the organization. In food chain pyramids, fully ninety percent of energy is lost from the system as heat; in organizational pyramids, a similarly massive amount of information, insight, and connectedness to customers is lost through each level of hierarchical separation.

Deliver to the Point of Value

In the human body, internal resources are automatically directed to the most vital parts of the body to sustain life. When someone is exposed to prolonged cold, nonessential functions are shut down in a logical progression to ensure that the brain and heart can survive. The body's fight-or-flight response kicks in when triggered by a perceived threat. Blood rushes to the head to maximize the brain's ability to process quickly. Adrenaline is fed to muscle groups in the legs and arms to run away or combat the potential threat. Evolution has been kind to our physical human bodies by making sure that our internal resources are prioritized and targeted to the precise locations where we will derive the greatest value in each situation.

Unfortunately, we have not evolved commensurately in how we organize ourselves in business. We do not concentrate our resources and prioritize our energy on the points of our organizations that deliver value to our customers. Conventional organizational design tends to funnel time and effort on internal, non-value activities. We dedicate teams of people, create reams of documents, and devote many person-years to preparing presentations for executives in oak-paneled conference rooms about ultimately inconsequential topics. At the same time, our customer service reps and sales teams face the daily wrath of frustrated customers. Leaders bleed over decisions about whether the company letterhead icon should be mauve or lavender while more finished goods are crammed into a warehouse full of other stuff we can't sell. People would not have survived long as a species if at the first sign of a saber-toothed tiger our bodies prioritized the flow of blood and hormones to our livers and tonsils instead of our hearts, leg muscles, and brains. It's crazy that we do the equivalent in our organizations every day.

Form over Function

Workers waste a lot of effort and suffer stress each day at work over the wrong things. Employees know that their jobs exist to serve customers. Given a choice, most would prefer to devote all of their professional energies to do what they can to meet their customers' needs. Unfortunately, workers are subjected to the imposition of requirements from managers that create little or no real value and distract employees from being able to focus on customers. As a result, workers often feel like the rope in a tug-of-war. They are torn between their desire to serve their customers and their fear of upsetting their managers by failing to address internal requirements of questionable value.

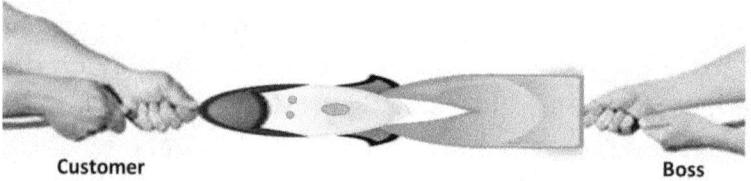

Customer　　　　　　　　　　　　　　　　　　　　Boss

The misappropriation of our effort and priority in the day-to-day operations of the business directly results from our organizational hierarchies. To show the relationship among roles and the focus of the organization, picture the conventional hierarchical pyramid in three dimensions as a conical shape. If we were to hover above the figure, looking down at the apex, it might look like a series of concentric circles.

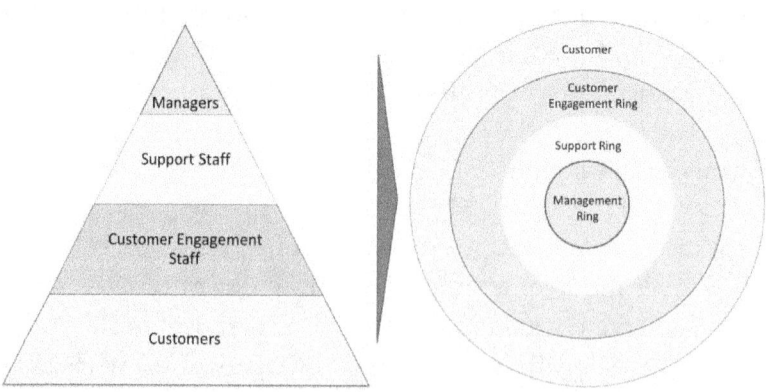

Law of Design

In this model, the focus of the organization lies in the center of the structure. Energy and resources are channeled toward the center in the same way that the sun's gravitational force makes it the center of our solar system.

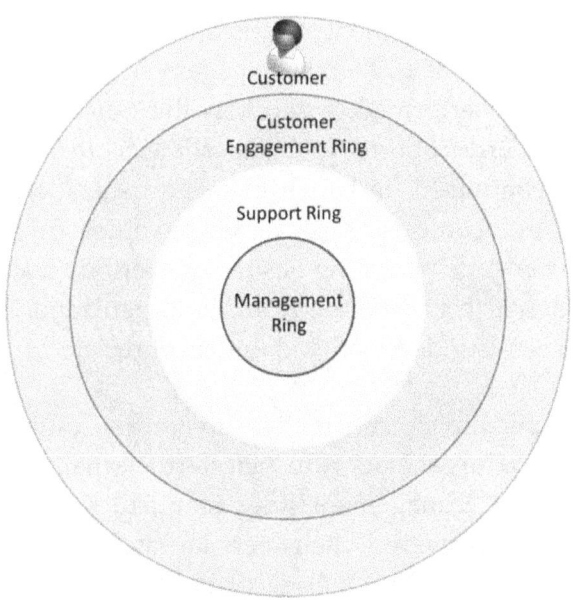

Like a model of the solar system, most organizations seem to rotate around the small cadre of executives, the Management Ring. The Management Ring is where macro decisions about the business are made, where strategic decisions and partnerships are rendered, where problems are escalated, and where people and resource needs are determined.

Beyond the Management Ring lies the Support Ring, comprised of support staff, equipment, and resources whose role it is to pass information between the Management Ring and the rest of the organization, and to sustain the basic infrastructure needs of the business. Finance, HR, Legal, IT, Security, Janitorial Services, etc., exist in this realm. The Support Ring provides little, if any, direct value to external customers, but exists to sustain the internal needs of the business.

The Customer Engagement Ring is the outermost area of the organization. In the Customer Engagement Ring are day-to-day activities performed by workers like Sales, Production, and Customer Support. Note that some of these activities might be conducted on behalf of our organizations by our partners and contractors. Beyond the outer orbit of the Customer Engagement Ring lies the mysterious realm of the Customer which is separate from the organization and all-too-often is misunderstood and underappreciated.

Most organizations principally direct the resources and energy of the organization to placate the small number of people in the Management Ring to make sure that their questions are answered, their fears are assuaged, and their orders are carried out. Job security depends on it. It is generally less dangerous for an employee's job security to irritate a one-off customer than to irritate an executive.

Most executives are so disengaged from the customer base, separated through layers of organizational rings, that they would be unlikely even to know of customer dissatisfaction until they are fed filtered spreadsheets and slide decks.

Middle managers float among the rings. They are the primary conduits of information, translating top-down executive demands into specific actions and passing status reports up the chain-of-command.

Imagine what would happen if we inverted the conventional organizational Ring model, and placed the Customer at the center of our business's solar system, empowering our customers with the same gravitational force and energy of the sun. Instead of channeling most of our energy on placating the Management Ring, we would focus our attention on delivering value to our customers, to those whose demands must be met in order for our business to survive.

We can also use the hierarchical ring framework to illustrate how much influence, resourcing, and focus each echelon in the organization has, based on the relative size of each ring. In many organizations, the Support Ring is bloated with internal, non-value bureaucracy that scavenges for nourishment and is self-perpetuating. The Management Ring gets most of the attention and effort and resources. The Customer Engagement Ring typically receives the least priority and consideration. Much of the attention customer-facing employees receive comes as squeezed commissions, draconian measures of effectiveness, and scrutiny for missing production targets. The Customer Engagement Ring may be treated like pure overhead instead of value-generating capacity. Sales, production, and customer service representatives are often the first to suffer from cost reduction efforts, and often experience more pressure to justify performance than Support Ring or Management Ring staff.

In the inverted model, the customer would take precedence within our organizational design. The importance of the Customer Engagement Ring, as the provider of value from our organization to the end customer of our goods and services, would be greatly increased. The Support Ring would lose precedence in this model. The functions within the Support Ring would focus more on enabling the Customer Engagement Ring to be successful and less on catering to the Management Ring. Finally, the Management Ring would find itself in the outer orbit of the organization, no longer the focus of the business. The purpose of the Management Ring would be to set longer-term strategy and to make sure that the Customer Engagement Ring receives the resources required to be successful.

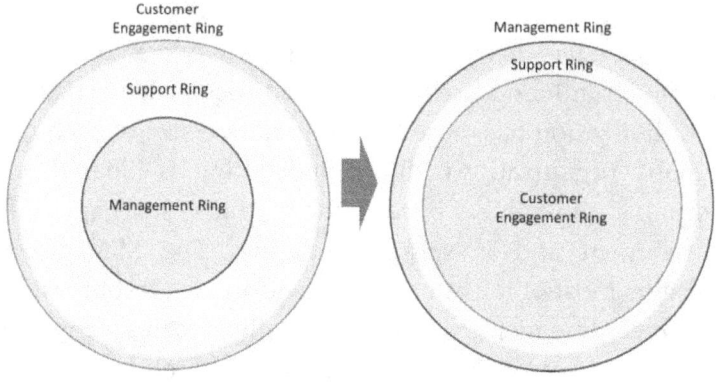

If we agree that the most successful organizations are more efficient and effective producers than their competitors, which model appears better positioned for success?

In the inverted model, those whose job it is to provide value to customers, to delight customers, learn from them, and observe competitive trends each day, are given every opportunity to excel. Do the sales staff need more training, better information, more resources? How responsive are marketers to real-time customer or competitor information being passed from the field? How reactive are marketers to revising collateral based on immediate feedback from the sales teams? How connected is R&D and product development to real-time feedback provided by the field teams and customer service representatives? How much of a typical executive's day is dedicated to internal meetings, slide deck reviews with consultants, and scorecard reviews versus on-the-ground interactions with customers and sales teams?

To illustrate the point, consider how elite Special Forces teams, such as Navy SEALs operate. Although small in number, these teams execute high precision, complex, and dangerous operations that require outstanding information, training, and resourcing to be successful. SEALs do not wade through mountains of bureaucracy to prepare for a mission, nor do they have to ask for authorization before conducting each phase of a mission. Much of their success depends on a nimble and responsive support team behind them to provide transportation to the mission site, equip them with the highest quality supplies in a timely manner, conduct the latest training as needed, and give accurate information. Missions are vetted and approved by leaders with more strategic vantage points and experience. The leaders' priority is to make sure that the SEALs are supported as much as possible to be successful. How different is that from the experience of the typical sales or customer service rep?

Redefining the Role of Managers

Note that the Customer Engagement Ring model requires that we reconsider what the role of a manager means. In the conventional hierarchical design, managers seldom, if ever, interact with customers. The Customer Engagement Ring is populated primarily by individuals with no management responsibility. Mid-level managers exist in the Support Ring as overseers of back office functions and as supervisors of the value producers in the Customer Engagement Ring. The

Management Ring is populated by the executive leaders, select members of the C-Suite, and their retinues of secretaries, consultants, and analysts.

In the conventional hierarchical model, the manager role description comprises one or more of the following five categories of responsibilities:

- *Decision-making and escalation*: Managers are empowered to decide the direction of their part of the business, to approve resource expenditures, and to resolve conflicts within their assigned purview.
- *Accountability enforcement*: Through some combination of threats, rewards, monitoring, and auditing, managers make sure that assigned workers are fulfilling their expected output within the prescribed rules and policies.
- *People development*: Through training or coaching, managers help workers to become more productive and correct substandard workers to meet minimum acceptable performance levels.
- *Resource stewardship*: Managers are expected to ensure that their assigned responsibilities are carried out without consuming resources of budget, inventory, and staff time beyond allocated levels.
- *Plan*: Some managers are expected to look ahead to plan for future growth next month, next year, and perhaps beyond.

In many businesses, these five role categories are restricted to designated people managers. The conventional paradigm that has remained intact since humans began organizing into societies considers people to be just another category of consumable resource. From this perspective, there's a certain logic to vesting combined authority and discretion over people, resources, and the direction of the organization exclusively in the same select group of designated leaders.

Most people selected for management positions, despite their skills or experience, are incapable of handling the scope of all five categories of management responsibilities. A manager might be proficient at some of the five management categories if he or she had prior experience with planning, project management, or resource tracking. Even for these managers, however, their abilities to plan, making decisions and manager resources are likely to become rusty over time. This is especially true as they distance themselves from the actual work and rely on delegates to do the work and report results.

What's more, for many in positions of formal authority over others, the people manager role is inextricably linked to ego. It feels empowering to hold others in a subjugated position, who have to do what you say and recognize your power through deferential behavior. We like to use terms such as "Alison works for me" and "Mark is under Jane in the org chart."

We refer to people as "resources" and quantify our importance by tallying the number of "heads" that report to us as we would servants or cattle. Workers aren't stupid and understandably resent this demeaning dynamic, which erodes the effectiveness of leadership.

As we have discussed, we need not look far to understand just how abysmal the track record of people management is today. Study after study attests that most people managers lack the soft skills to add value to workers assigned to them.

Let's examine each of the five management categories to understand how they perpetuate the backwards leadership-centric perspective:

Fiction 1: Only managers should make decisions.

To be clear, it is necessary in most organizations to have designated people empowered with the accountability and responsibility to make specific decisions. This is particularly so when differing perspectives require one person to resolve escalations and make the final determination. Decision-making by committee can be a great way to enhance collaboration and a wider sense of ownership, but decision-making by consensus is also time-consuming and inefficient.

That said, many organizations fail to understand the fine line between empowering leaders to decide in the interest of efficiency and the damaging results of managers who oversubscribe their decision-making role through micromanagement and lack of consideration for other perspectives. When managers insert themselves onto the critical path of those workers whose job it is to deliver value to customers, they create unnecessary delays and bottlenecks of bureaucracy, queues for approval, and demoralization of capable workers who feel powerless and demeaned. Micromanagement also sends a clear signal to employees that they are not trustworthy, intelligent, or capable enough to carry out their assigned tasks without the guiding intervention of managers. When managers fail to consider input from workers when making decisions, whether through arrogance, ignorance, or expedience, they become their own weakest link. They are unable to contribute to the organization beyond the limits of their individual limitations.

Organizations that promote centralized authority, in which employees are expected to seek approval for most decisions, handicap their potential to be nimble and innovate.

As much as possible, decision-making should be delegated to where the information lies. This drives rapid responses by those who have the clearest perspective and understanding of the situation and the impact on customers. For example, a proven, balanced approach to decision-making is for managers to exercise what enlightened military organizations call "commander's intent." By this approach, leaders establish clear goals and guidelines, and then trust that staff will use their judgment and skills to carry out the details of realizing the objectives. Commander's intent recognizes that those closest to the action are best positioned to make the tactical decisions needed to execute the plan. Front-line troops are trained, empowered, and trusted to excel. The practice of commander's intent maximizes the strategic utility of a manager as policy maker. It also maximizes and grows the skills and resourcefulness of those tasked with achieving the objectives of the organization.

Fiction 2: Managers are needed for accountability.

Imagine a place where each worker is competent and honest enough to be trusted to do the right thing for the business and to do it well. In this nirvana, there would be no need to check employees through various monitoring activities that are expected to be part of the manager's role.

Of course, we do not live in nirvana, and people are imperfect. This unfortunate reality leads to one of two options to drive proficiency and responsibility for workers to get the right things done well. You may believe the effort that workers apply is commensurate with the level of scrutiny by overseers, in which case the conventional role of manager as auditor is the right one for you.

However, you may believe that employees who are trusted and empowered, and who share a sense of ownership for the optimal outcome of the organization, will do the right thing. If so, you understand how much more effective and less patronizing it would be to have a system in which everybody holds themselves and each other accountable. By entrusting workers with the expectations of quality production, we replace the patronizing us-versus-them message (that says managers are needed to force people to do the right thing) with a message of trust and empowerment. Since people are imperfect and mistakes will happen, any activity needed to monitor production and efficiency is focused on the process itself. Improvement of team dynamics is prioritized over scrutiny of people. When bonuses reflect shared outcomes, then workers have an incentive to hold themselves more accountable so they do not let their peers down. They hold one another more accountable because their personal outcome partially depends on the work of others.

Note that empowering teams to be more responsible for their work doesn't absolve employees of being held to standards of performance and conduct. Workers who need additional training should be identified by their teams. Workers who for whatever reason fail to adhere to the standards of conduct should be disciplined or dismissed. Managers should teach teams how to be more accountable rather than wasting effort in a self-defeating game of gotcha. On empowered teams with shared incentives, it is in the worker's interest and the organization's interest for workers to hold themselves and their peers to high standards.

Consider the extreme example of front-line infantry troops under fire. Combat veterans often say that their primary motivation for facing death and enduring deprivation was not related to orders administered by officers or even a sense of self-preservation. The primary motivation was to make sure they did not let their buddies down. This argues for a system in which responsibility, which is essential to a high-functioning team, should be decentralized as much as possible and made a part of each worker's expectations.

Fiction 3: Managers should take it upon themselves to lead employee professional development.

People are living things that need respect and empowerment to grow and thrive. Consider how much of our lives we dedicate to our professional activities. It's natural for people to want to invest in themselves to contribute more value and to gain more knowledge. It's also in the interest of most organizations to want to invest in employees so they can be better contributors.

Enlightened learning organizations realize that there are always opportunities to drive more efficiencies and increase effectiveness. Continuous improvement means that all people must become learners. Learning organizations stress team problem solving.

The issue isn't whether people development is a worthwhile investment—of course it is. The question is, what is the optimal way to develop people?

Here's the answer: often managers tasked with developing others have neither the skills to train others nor the credibility to do so. Even managers who are skilled trainers may not be able to drive constructive development outcomes for their employees if workers are distracted by the ego tug-of-war or posturing inherent in some manager-employee relationships.

There are three common avenues that can help employees develop professionally, none of which needs to be included as part of a manager's direct responsibilities. First, organizations might invest in hiring professional trainers who can impart specific expertise to employees. Second, some employees find value in developing ongoing relationships with an experienced mentor, a person with much deeper expertise and experience, who can provide wisdom and technical guidance. Remember that the role of mentor and the role of people manager are mutually exclusive. Finally, each individual must be responsible for seeking opportunities for his or her own professional development, such as certification programs or online classes.

Note that in all three examples of professional development roles, there is no requirement that a manager must be involved. While some managers with particular subject matter expertise might be able to contribute to training programs, it's possible that vesting a people manager with professional development responsibilities may impede the professional development process. Good managers will support professional development while realizing their own limitations in providing training to workers.

Fiction 4: Managers are needed to enforce proper stewardship of the organization's resources.

Most organizations account for resources like budget and inventories by cascading responsibility through the chain of command. Thus promoting the responsible consumption of resources and yielding the highest return on investment. In reality, however, since most managers are not directly involved in value creation and do not consume many resources, they are in the uncomfortable position of being accountable for resources that others are using. This means that managers can only influence responsible resource management and consumption through carrots and sticks.

Effective resource management means that responsibility for resources must be invested at the point of usage. If employees who consume, store, track, and order resources do not feel this ownership, then there is little incentive for them to be responsible. If ownership is solely vested in managers who are disassociated with direct engagement in any aspect of resource management, then nobody really has responsibility. As a result, obligation for responsible resource usage should be part of each employee's job description. While managers cannot delegate their own accountability, they should require employees to treat resources with the same care and attention they would if the employees were owners of the business because they have a vested interest in the organization's success. When business is good, workers have stable income. When business is not doing well, employees lose the security of a reliable paycheck.

Fiction 5: Only managers can drive strategic planning.

A common role for managers is to look over the horizon to develop near-term, mid-term, and long-term strategic objectives and execution plans. In fact, in many organizations it is assumed that individual contributors handle tactical execution, while managers focus on strategic direction. With this bifurcated perspective comes the hierarchical assumption that daily value delivery to customers is lowly work that should be resigned to the rank and file; longer-term strategic planning requires the intellectual horsepower and insight that only managers have.

Business literature often complains that the vast majority of strategy efforts are miserable failures. It is difficult to develop usable strategies. Few organizations translate strategies into meaningful plans that can cascade through the organization. Most attempts at strategic planning result in colorful but useless presentations that are never fully implemented, do not achieve stated goals, and are rarely shared with or understood by employees. If strategic planning is supposed to be an inherent core competency of managers and yet the vast majority of strategic planning efforts fail, it would seem most managers lack the skills or experience to develop and execute strategies. The ability to develop successful strategies is not magically realized when one assumes a managerial title.

Effective strategic planning requires the expertise of those who work with customers closely and are experts in the means of production. Leaders in the organization should play a central role in weighing strategic alternatives about the direction of the company; however, to ignore the perspectives of employees when developing strategic plans is to deprive the organization of the benefit of the most valuable insight.

In our experience, most annual strategic planning exercises are little more than a block-checking ritual or an executive echo chamber. The ideal way to drive meaningful, measurable, and actionable strategic planning that is understood and owned by the entire organization is to engage all staff in the strategy development process. We recommend investigating the Lean strategy deployment (A3) approach.

Role of Leaders

What real value do managers provide in a typical organization? Expressed another way, how much of what managers do would customers be willing to pay for? How many management roles in our hierarchical structure come from a sense of entitlement for years of dedication to the company? How often is a manager's title the reward for so many late nights and indignities endured to get ahead? How many people manager roles are manufactured as a prerequisite of a forced-fit template career trajectory through middle management? If we agree that bad managers are destructive and the best managers are those who listen to and empower already capable employees, it questions what value these managers serve. In the interest of the business, how much non-value-producing management overhead is acceptable?

We do not advocate abolishing all manager roles. However, most of the functions assigned to managers can and should be vested in employees who work closest to where value is created. Most organizations would benefit by investing in developing the capabilities, collaboration, and ownership of their employees so that the overhead burden of a management tier that consumes a disproportionate amount of resources without providing corresponding value would no longer be required.

To illustrate the point, we are reminded of a consulting engagement with an insurance organization. The company experienced a significant increase in claims volume but due to budget constraints couldn't hire additional agents to process the claims. As a result, the average processing time for claims increased. This produced a degraded customer experience and massive cost increases to the company, since older claims correlated to the increase of additional expensive complicating factors over the life of a claim.

Like many companies, this organization blindly followed the conventional approach of promoting the most productive and experienced claims agents into supervisory roles of each claims unit. The result was a systematic brain drain of the most talented employees from direct value-generating activity into administrative tasks like attending meetings and reviewing reports. The closest these supervisors came to the point of value generation was to conduct hundreds of claims audits each month, only a small percentage of which were defective.

Besides various improvements to streamline the processes, one of the easiest and most impactful recommendations we made was to replace the unit supervisor role with low-cost administrators. To maximize the value of the supervisors, while mitigating a potential sense of demotion, the supervisors returned to productive service in the claims units, where they processed the most sensitive and challenging cases. They were also assigned to mentor more junior claims managers to share their experience. The twenty-five claims units combined into eight units. Each unit assigned a lower-cost administrator to manage the necessary overhead support requirements for the claims managers. Many of the administrative tasks once conducted by the supervisors simply vanished, and nobody missed them. Soon after the reassignment of the supervisors, productivity, quality, and unit morale soared to the highest levels ever experienced in the company.

The responsibilities expected of most managers could either be vested in productive employees at the point of value creation or could cease altogether. The remaining useful managerial activities should be handled by a few appointed leaders in order to:

- Drive efficient decision-making in the interest of the entire company, since consensus-based decision-making across an organization is almost always impractical and biased by tactical viewpoints. Escalated concerns and hard trade-off decisions should be made by objective and experienced managers with the full perspective of the organization.
- Set a strategic direction that evaluates the entire landscape of the enterprise, including future trends, partnerships, new market opportunities, and competitive threats.
- Serve as ambassadors to executive customers, partners, and stakeholders to negotiate terms in the highest interest of the organization.
- Allocate limited resources to maximize the delivery of value to customers, which includes budget, equipment, employee compensation, and professional development.
- Help to establish and preserve the organization's values and culture.

By shrinking the support and leadership concentric rings in our organizations, we will empower those who create and deliver value to customers. This, in turn, will shift greater focus to the customer.

Survival Guide

What does your organization's concentric Ring Model look like?

- Do you include customers in your organizational model?
- How much time and resources are spent by staff to produce and report presentations for leadership teams about the status of the organization?
- What is the Support Ring cost-per-unit of what your organization produces? In other words, what proportion of your overall budget is assigned to support staff and equipment that do not directly contribute to the delivery of value to the customer?
- What is the Management Ring cost-per-unit of what your organization produces? In other words, what proportion of your overall budget is assigned to support leadership (e.g. administrative support, compensation and perks, and analyst staff) that does not directly contribute to the delivery of value to the customer?
- What activities do executives perform day-to-day that a customer would not be willing to pay for? What valuable executive activities and decisions could be delegated to middle managers or workers?
- What activities do middle managers perform day-to-day that a customer would not be willing to pay for? What valuable management activities and decisions could be delegated to workers?
- What are five ways you could improve responsiveness to needs of staff in the Customer Engagement Ring (such

as reducing approval layers, increasing local approval thresholds, or increasing allocation of budget to customer-serving activities)?

Law of Attraction and Neglect

If absolute power corrupts absolutely, does
absolute powerlessness make you pure?
-Harry Shearer

4 | *What You Don't See or Hear Can Kill You*

Anglerfish thrive in the deep ocean by using as a lure a modified dorsal fin that protrudes over its mouth like a fishing pole. At the tip is a bulb-like organ filled with luminous bacteria, perfect for enticing unsuspecting prey in the dark waters. When victims swim near, the anglerfish swallows them whole, and can devour prey up to twice its size.

In the natural world, appearances can be part of hunting strategy. King cobras, the largest of venomous snakes, are the same color as the ground and can lie immobile for hours, until striking and ingesting another snake, lizard, or rodent that passes by. Male peacocks rely on a flowery appearance to attract a mate and perpetuate the species. Appearances can be used as a defense, as in camouflage, like zebra stripes in tall grass. Evolution tells us that appearances are not designed, but evolve. If evolutionary changes work, the species continues. If they don't, it's adios, often violently.

In the business world, appearances are designed but operate the same way as in nature; appearances work and the business continues to open its doors, or they don't work, with fatal results. Unfortunately, it is a rare business that understands appearances as a new Darwinian law of survival.

The Power Suit

Take wearing a two-button or three-button business suit, for example. Who wears a suit, and what does it mean? Social evolution tells the story. Men's clothing slowly changed from the courtly formal clothes of seventeenth-century English nobility we're all familiar with, through military uniforms, to more tailored attire like the morning coat. What we put our arms into this morning is merely an accident of time. Why we wear what we do, however, is a calculated message, and one with consequences.

Emily Chertoff, writing in *Businessweek*, describes her preferred attire as having the "fashion sensibility of an eighty-year-old man," the power suit, black and bland, female version. Hers is a blazer, button-down shirt, slacks, and high heels. Her suit makes her feel powerful; but better yet, she says, it projects the image that this woman cannot be taken for granted. "That's why it's called a power suit," she adds.

This reality of expression and perception is important enough to stimulate academic research to understand the ramifications. One study is "Ritual Costumes and Status Transition: the Female Business Suit as Totemic Emblem," by Michael R. Solomon and Punam Anand, both of New York University. Among the findings is the concept of "I wear, therefore I am," and the idea that for some businesswomen, the totem of the business suit far outweighs any interest in fashion. The authors say, for example,

> Like men, these women now realize that clothing is vital to the communication of credibility, competence, achievement and professionalism. This goal often dictates criteria which would be anathema to the stereotypic fashion plate: Conformity, standardization, sensibility, drabness—in short, the business uniform.

Academics also reference Betty Harragan, who reports that:

> An executive's work clothes are not guided by comfort, looks, attractiveness, taste or novelty—they are responses to the dress orders of the day. His voluntary compliance can be crucial to his success. Upcoming women are also being judged for future potential on the basis of dress. The trouble is, nobody knows what criteria to use—not men or women, not management policy-makers...

Research suggests a jacket is necessary for both sexes to project power and status. Skirts may be a bit more difficult to portray maleness and power, but those who make the attempt seem to be successful.

The more someone has to lose by not fitting in, the more important it is to understand what is expected and do exactly that. The more someone wants to fit in, the more they will do whatever it takes. The right clothes act as a symbolic exoskeleton against social missteps. Freud might say that such behavior is the person defending herself by identifying with the aggressor; maybe it's a version of Stockholm syndrome.

Clothing performs more duties than to protect us from stares and the weather. Here is how the power suit works:

- A jacket's square shoulders exaggerate the size and strength of the torso.
- The jacket's length enlarges the upper body.
- The boxy structure of the suit hides fine movements, which masks shrugs of uncertainty or submissiveness.
- The arms of a suit jacket can cover many ills and increase perceived arm strength.
- Dark suit colors, the darker the better, project authority.
- Darker shades project a serious, formal look.
- Navy is the preferred color in the corporate world, less forbidding than total black, conveying a calm and pleasant mood.
- As for other colors, plaid is scattered, yellows too lighthearted, total black too intense, brown too sad and untrustworthy, and light gray not substantial enough.
- The sharper the tailoring, the more formidable the wearer.

The power suit is not just a concept. It is a living totem of how business people interact. It symbolizes the power of controlling how people work with one another.

The Power Tie

What's a power suit without a power tie? Red is the color of the power tie. This symbol defines the wearer of a power suit as the embodiment of you-better-watch-out-because-you-are-not-going-to-win attitude. The red tie is not as dramatic as an alpha male with giant muscles, sans shirt and with crossed bandoliers across his chest, sweating and brandishing two assault weapons, but it might well be the corporate office equivalent, visually displaying the man in control.

The power tie adds the last, necessary touch to the power suit. For males, it is an overt phallus we wear brazenly around our necks for all the world to see. We laugh at flamboyant displays of masculinity in nature, yet it is difficult to find a more garish illustration of power-sexuality than the ubiquitous power tie.

Trappings of Power

Designed appearances often extend beyond personal clothing. Consider the stereotypical executive chamber, an immaculate and sterile sanctuary set apart from the cluttered and noisy production cubicle villages. Like a frontline combat compound, executives are protected by concentric lines of security. The executive offices are clustered on the top floor along the windows, colocated in the same hall. Attentive secretaries sit like bodyguards before walls of marble or heavy wood. Penetrate the sanctuary further and you'll encounter individual executive offices protected behind closed doors and louvered windows. Hallways may attest to the lineage of greatness of past leaders, captured in photos or painted portraits on the wall. Enter an office and you'll see a large desk interposed between you and the occupant like a mahogany redoubt.

All the usual artifacts of leadership in most organizations serve two primary functions. The first is to preserve a sense of privacy for the manager by screening him from the unnecessary distractions of the business and the customers. What these layers of screens do in reality is further isolate the manager from the operations of the business and the voice of the customer. Well-appointed offices might feel like luxurious wombs, but they are really tasteful echo chambers that can cut the executives off from the reality of the business.

The second function of the trappings of power is to create an aura of prestige and authority. This provides executives with a psychological advantage over customers and partners by impressing them with a glossy veneer of power that masks the person's natural inadequacies. Trappings are also designed to intimidate lower-ranked managers and employees. Employees will fear the status of the executive even if the character and capability of the executive do not warrant respect.

Trappings of power and influence in business are examples of how appearances can intimidate and isolate people from the real responsibility of engagement.

Fatalities

Power suits themselves don't actually hurt anyone and, uncomfortable as they may be, ties are not directly harmful either. What causes the problem is the dynamic they set up: us against them, you against me, me afraid of you, and you afraid of me.

For over twenty years, experts in Lean Thinking (the Toyota Production System) have been trying to apply the classic Seven Wastes of production to how people interact. In their pioneering article "Two Great Wastes," Greg Howell and Hal Macomber presented not listening and not speaking as a cause of considerable interpersonal waste. Ask yourself,

"Why wouldn't someone speak up?" And "What is lost if someone doesn't speak up?"

Not speaking up caused the deadliest air disaster in history, when two loaded 747 jumbo jets collided in the fog on the island of Tenerife, March 27, 1977, claiming the lives of 583 people.

Because of a bomb threat at the main airport of the Canary Islands, many planes filled with tourists had to detour to the small airport at Tenerife. With too many planes and not enough airport, jumbo jets stacked up all around. To make matters worse, fog stopped all traffic.

Senior KLM pilot Jacob Van Zanten knew what a delayed takeoff meant: his crew would be over their allowed hours, a new crew would be needed, crew and passengers would have to be put up overnight, and his plane would be unmanned and thus out of service. He needed to get his plane into the air. Then the fog began to lift in many places. Two planes were to taxi down the runway, turn, with one exiting the runway and the other, the KLM, holding until cleared for takeoff.

Communication with the tower from both planes was confusing and nonstandard. The Pan Am, still out of sight, reported it was not yet off the runway at the same time the control tower told the KLM that it had route clearance (not takeoff clearance). Assuming he was cleared for takeoff, the captain pushed the throttle forward and the plane raced down the fog-shrouded runway. First Officer Meurs reminded the captain they did not have clearance. The captain ignored Meurs, and the first officer did not press the issue. None of the crew wanted to insult the senior member in the cockpit.

At almost takeoff speed, Van Zanten suddenly saw the KLM in the middle of the runway and all he could do was to leapfrog the other plane. The KLM jet lifted off, but only high enough to slice through the center of the Pan Am, taking off its entire top section. The KLM slammed into the earth, and the Pan Am exploded in flames. All on the KLM died, sixty-one on the Pan Am survived, including the entire cockpit crew.

Air industry expert and pilot John Nance summarized what happened: "Ultimately, the reason that that KLM aircraft began rolling down that fog shrouded runway was this was a team, but it wasn't allowed to operate like a team. So one man made a mistake and that mistake stuck."

Nance took the lessons from aviation and applied them to medicine in his book *Why Hospitals Should Fly*, about a fictional Denver hospital. He shows how safety processes and tools pioneered in the airline industry can work in medicine, such as checklists, timeouts, repeating orders, and team dynamics that override power hierarchies.

Uniforms, Dress Codes, and Casual Friday

A uniform, by intent, is to turn many into one. It also defines "What I do is who I am," such as a doctor or a judge. The opposite of a uniform is distinctive dress that declares, "I am a unique individual and will do things my way." In the business world, what you want is appearance that says, "I'm capable and willing" to do the task at hand.

Uniforms can portray a sense of professionalism and competence if the uniform entails an identity and code of behavior, such as marines, firefighters, and nurses. When these people don their uniforms, they become one of the many who are one with a sense of pride, responsibility, and presumed credentials. Experiments have shown that wearing a uniform can change behavior. One example is that wearing a lab coat improved experimental subjects' attention to detail. When the same coat was called a painter's coat, it didn't improve attention to detail.

A uniform without an identity and code of behavior is worthless or worse. Such a uniform has no purpose except for control. We know of one manager who demanded that his employees "look sharp," as he did every day in his power suit. The expected uniform was a tie and a coat when attending meetings. It soon became apparent to those who worked for him that he was all hat and no cattle; he had little knowledge in his area, little leadership ability, and even less management skill. Soon, all who worked for him mocked his dress and his insistence on looks. Instead of the pride he was looking for, by such a strong and empty focus on appearance with no underlying professional credibility he created the opposite: a disengaged workforce.

Uniforms should be distinctive, create a sense of pride and belonging, and most importantly for business, define expected behavior.

The same can happen with dress codes. These are often created by leadership so employees will "look professional." When promoted by fiat, dress codes are resented by most employees, at least those who act and dress like grown-ups. If most employees are dressing appropriately all by themselves, those few who don't should be taken aside and educated. If, however, the dress code is designed for specific purposes, such as impressing customers, this creates meaning and identity and the dress code works very much like a uniform.

Depending on desired outcomes, uniforms and dress codes have to be balanced with promoting individuality. Branded behavior, like that found at Disneyland and many upscale hotels, demands uniformity that is often supported by uniforms and dress codes. On the other hand, most organizations would benefit from employees being empowered and encouraged to innovate and improve. Kristi Blicharski, an empowerment coach, says it is important to encourage individuality because it promotes confidence and creativity. "Studies have shown," she says, "that when we look good on the outside, we feel good on the inside, and what's important to recognize is that everyone has their own unique feelings about what makes them look and feel their best. Why try to inhibit that?"

Some places try to balance the need to maintain appearance standards with a more relaxed environment by having what are known as casual Fridays. The idea behind casual Friday was to lessen the strict dress codes of the week to improve morale, create a more relaxed atmosphere, have a little fun, encourage individuality, and maybe even enhance creativity. In many places, casual Friday means wearing clothes just one level below the norm. For example, in places that require coats and ties, casual Friday might mean blazers without a tie. In settings where polo shirts are worn all the time, T-shirts might bloom on Fridays. Some casual places do the opposite and have dress-up Fridays. It's all to get out of the rut that can be made by mandating the clothes we wear. Maybe we shouldn't be in a rut in the first place.

So whom do we dress for?

- Our individual selves?
- Our professional identity?
- Our boss?

- Our job?
- Our company?
- Our customers?
- The job we want to have?

Wouldn't that be an interesting discussion to have with employees?

The bottom line on uniforms, dress codes, and casual Fridays is that appearances can make a huge difference in the day-to-day functioning of a business. If you want uniformity of purpose, choose uniforms and dress codes. More casual approaches seem to work better if you're seeking more individuality and creativity. No matter what your purpose, look at appearances with a purposeful eye. If you instill a dress code, what cost/benefit are you creating? What is the desired improved behavior and what are employees giving up and getting? What barriers are you creating?

The Back Stairs and Other Deadly Traps

When you're away from the public areas of a business and are where the employees walk the hallways, have you noticed how mucky the back stairs are? The stairs may be clean, but are often stained with spilled coffee, the walls are painted a dull gray, and the walk itself echoes with each footstep. Back stairs are utilitarian, designed and built to work, not to be pleasing. Their appearance is one of indifference and neglect. What's the message to employees?

There are many ways the appearance of the workplace can damage your business. One organization we recently visited was polished to a high sheen. Everything was modern, designed to be neat and tidy to the *n*th degree. Each floor was identical in design but had graphics picked specifically for that floor's particular work. Desks, walls, windows, workstations, meeting rooms, and everything else was designed for maximum neatness and efficiency. We were reminded of the town of Stepford and wondered if all people who worked in this place had become an automaton performer. It seemed that way.

Interior space design can alter mood and behavior and is rarely used to advantage; rather, it is often neglected or even misused.

Place seating too close together and you create stress, emotional and physical, possibly leading to irritation, depressed mood, and physical illness. The wrong colors can make people anxious or bored. Provocative lines and colors can invigorate. A well-appointed workplace means you care; a dump means you don't. Another thought is that if you realize how your company is short-changing staff and you decide to remodel, ask for their input and use it.

The first place we like to visit when asked to assess an organization is the restroom. Unlike the meticulous reception area or conference rooms, the humble restroom will reveal how much care and ownership employees really feel for the organization. This basest of office facilities will show in no uncertain terms either attention to detail, courtesy for colleagues, and personal ownership, or will scream apathy, contempt, or worse. Break rooms are similar litmus tests.

The Front of the House

It isn't rocket science to understand that pleasing customers is the smoothest and widest road to success. Yet examples abound of companies failing to perform even the basics—a clean, neat, inviting place where customers feel welcomed and become eager to buy what you have to sell.

We watched the TV reality show *Restaurant: Impossible* to learn about what to avoid. Chef Robert Irvine is invited by failing restaurants to save them through two days of problem-solving with a budget of ten thousand dollars. Without fail, Chef Robert discovers two classic problems: the restaurant is filthy and the owners haven't noticed; and the restaurant is ugly and/or boring and the owners have gotten used to that and have failed to notice that part too.

Most of these restaurants have lost money for a few years, have been in the family for a long time, and the owners seem paralyzed to figure out what to do. To the rescue comes Chef Robert, who walks through the front door and immediately points out the dirt on the ceiling fans, the outdated décor, rips in the fabric seating, dusty wall hangings, and a floor with decades of ground-in dirt.

Chef Robert does a deep cleaning and his designer comes up with a new look that says, "We're glad you're here, welcome." He also reduces the menu and improves the food, but first on his list is always cleanliness and attractiveness; blind spots to the owners that are killing their business.

In a similar vein is another reality show to prove the point: *Hotel Impossible*, with hotelier Anthony Melchiorri. Same approach: clean up what's dirty and fix the décor. He arrives by car and has trouble finding either a place to park or the front desk. Along the way, if he spots a damaged fence, door, or fixture, it's his practice to break it completely so it has to be repaired. He inspects the room, tearing apart the bed to find bedbugs, nails, and caterpillars. He then moves on to the bathroom, where in many shows he will gag and almost vomit at the filth.

In both programs, the concept is that unless leadership creates a functional working environment and has clear standards, objectives, and expectations, the business will slowly— or sometimes alarmingly quickly—sink.

A filthy and boring environment can come in many guises. For example, a meeting with extraneous conversation, interruptions, unclear rules, too many attendees, and a poor agenda has its own kind of filth. This is the kind that discourages people from speaking up when they have a good idea. Like any muck, mismanaged meetings and other interactions soon lead to a lack of interest and avoidance, which leads to inattention or anger, which leads to a broken and soon-to-die business.

Survival Guide

Invite an objective outsider unfamiliar with your office to visit and show them around to conduct an honest appraisal of what they see. Ask them to answer the following questions:

- Can you tell what hierarchical position a person has, based on their clothes?
- Does size, design, or placement of working space indicate what hierarchical position a person has?
- How many levels of physical barriers do you observe between staff and an executive in her chair?
- Are leaders physically separated from the areas where value is being generated and delivered to customers? If so, how much separation is there?
- Does the working environment indicate that people take pride and ownership in working there?
- Does the state of the restroom indicate that people take pride and ownership in working there?
- Does the state of the common kitchen, break room, or lounge area indicate that people take pride and ownership in working there?
- From the appearance of the office, does this seem like a place you would be comfortable working and could do your best work?

Law of the Living Dead

I like zombie movies. I like *The Walking Dead*; I like the metaphor of it, simply because when we go with the zombie concept—if you're bitten by a zombie, you don't transform into something else like a vampire or a werewolf or what-ever. You become something that's not you.
-Marilyn Manson

5 | *Zombie Companies Create Zombie Workers*

As you probably know, a zombie is a human corpse brought back to life, usually by an evil entity. A zombie spends its time stumbling in clumsy pursuit of attractive, scantily clad young women, the bumbling sidekicks of heroes, the heroes themselves, and the odd innocent bystander with the sole intent of devouring them. No one likes zombies; they are ugly, mean, and not a lot of fun. As a rule, zombies don't plan, they are not empathetic (thinking only of themselves), and they produce nothing of value.

Zombies have no working heart. They just go about their business of eating living humans. They have no other intentions. Zombies do not think about a greater good. They don't innovate. Zombies are a total waste. Another interesting fact about zombies is that they are unaware of the cost of their single-mindedness. In their quest to devour living humans, they can get arms and legs shot off and think nothing of it.

Zombies, unlike people, are invulnerable. People have feelings, physical and emotional needs, wishes, and fears. In environments where any feelings have to be suppressed, people are dehumanized. Zombies wouldn't care. They can rise again after a shotgun blast, even one to the heart. Because they do not have an operational heart, using it is impossible and losing it is no problem

Zombies are also a virus, always adding new members to their ranks through their contaminated bites. In no time at all, just one zombie can lead to a pandemic of mindless, flesh-eating, undead beings.

Zombie companies are similar. Zombie companies are animated, responding to their environment, but are essentially dead inside, rotting from the top down. Zombie companies care about only two numbers—revenue and expenses—both signs of self-serving consumption. Revenue is created by devouring the resources of customers, and expenses are the costs of gobbling up resources, including employees. Consumption isn't necessarily a bad thing; all creatures, living and undead, consume resources to convert into energy. The difference between living creatures and the undead, however, is that whereas living creatures do other things than just eat, like procreate, evolve, and even create, zombies serve no purpose other than to consume.

Zombie companies think only of what is good right now for owners. Long-term planning is a concept outside their immediate hunger. Zombie companies are animated by the bottom line, and are slaves to their shareholders. Although few people have the power to animate dead people, many managers can create zombie organizations, zombie departments, and zombie employees. And in the classic zombie model, the zombie contagion can spread fast through an organization. All it takes is a single bad manager or self-serving employee in a culture with no cultural antibodies to defend itself, and the zombification of the company can become all-consuming.

Experts estimate that between thirty and sixty percent of businesses are zombie companies, the chance of being a zombie company increasing with the organization's size. This means that the larger the company, the more likely it is to be a zombie company. Since larger companies employ more people, a large number of employees work for zombie companies. This equates to between twenty and fifty million zombies roaming the corridors of commerce, non-profits, and government agencies in the United States alone, at any one time. The graph below explains the percentages:

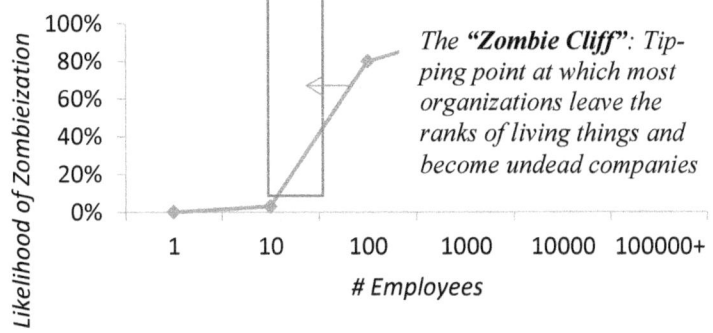

As you can see from the graph, a single proprietor business has little chance of being a zombie organization. This is because the single owner has to relate to others well to run the business, something impossible for a zombie. The single person also has to work to grow the business and to make changes on the fly when necessary. A zombie single owner business will soon fail.

Small businesses are often family businesses. Families are the opposite of zombies. There are often intense emotions expressed and dealt with in a family enterprise. Zombies may exist in a family business, but in almost all instances, the zombie member is expelled or infects all others.

Non-family small businesses are like family in that there are direct connections between manager, workers, and customers. Even without the emotional overlay of a family, small businesses are often known for being a tightknit group, like birds flying in unison. Communication is direct, feelings usually open, and the health and direction of the business well known to all. Once the business is ongoing, employees often stay for decades. There is often a sense of mutual responsibility for one another in a small business, a sensibility alien to zombies.

As a business grows, however, defects in the structure allow toxins to infiltrate, invisible at first, but causing great damage. The toxin is dehumanization (zombification), taking many forms.

Micromanagement and Sycophancy

Both authors have consulted at non-profits, places where you might think everyone was touchy-feely and un-zombie-like. However, that is not always the case. At one, a manager exhibited a classic form of zombification: micromanagement. He was intelligent and driven to do the best work and create optimal results. He approved all things down to the least important slide in a PowerPoint deck. This resulted in his staff focusing not on the actual work, but on keeping the boss happy.

The desire to please, receive praise, and stay out of trouble suppressed independent thinking. These employees were becoming zombies, disposable in the boss's quest for good-looking outcomes. A boss who incites this behavior in any way becomes an internal, zombifier of employees.

Meetings that Waste Time (which is to say, most meetings)

Stand in a random hallway of most corporations and you'll see hordes of stiff-limbed, bleary-eyed, incoherent employees lumbering out of conference rooms each hour on the hour, like so many zombies squinting painfully at the hint of daylight. It's easy to see that meetings are one of the greatest causes of zombification. Conference rooms are like undead incubators that purge the life force and creativity out of employees. People are numb to the reality that the countless hours they invest in reviewing projected slides and staring blankly at conference phones result in little benefit to anyone. University of Minnesota research suggests that upwards of fifty percent of meeting time is unproductive. *Industry Week* called meetings "the great white collar crime" that wastes thirty-seven billion dollars a year. Too bad their estimate is measured in dollars. It would have been more enlightening if they had measured zombification.[1]

Absence of Recognition

Another poisonous source is the absence of appreciation for hard work. Zombies don't recognize the good in others; they just want to eat their brains. Many times a day, the good work the average worker is doing goes unnoticed and unheralded. A receptionist's smile, for example, can make a

---

[1] This may be paranoid, but there has been talk of computers taking over the world. Think about this for a minute. Work slides are computer generated. These slides are ubiquitous in boring meetings. Is there a sinister connection between computers, slide-driven meetings, and zombification?

world of difference for a nervous patient first entering a medical office. A defective manager might counter that the receptionist was just doing the job as defined in the job description and is sufficiently rewarded by receiving a paycheck. Recognition doesn't have to be formal; in fact, small gestures of appreciation often mean more than manufactured awards like plaques.

Useless Work

How about the effect of doing dumb work? Ask employees if some of their work is dumb and each one will have at least one example of work that seems to have no value. There are two possibilities, neither good: One is that they are asked to do work that makes no sense; the other is that they haven't learned or been told that the work has value. In either instance, the employee is treated as an unfeeling zombie.

Similarly, boring work is a slow and painful zombified death.

And so is a work environment that brings no joy. Active humans are a bounty of emotions. To suppress emotions is to be partially dead. To work in an environment devoid of life voids life.

Avoiding Conflict

Conflict is impossible to avoid when people work together. However, it is possible, and likely, that conflict is ignored in most work environments. Employees aren't sure how to raise a concern without sounding like complainers, which is a bad thing to be. Many managers would rather ignore conflict than address it, knowing they are good at ignoring and not so good at resolving. Zombies don't have conflicts among themselves; treating employees as if they don't have concerns simply to avoid conflict means you're treating them like zombies.

Managers often do another bit of avoidance that fosters zombification by not addressing performance issues with the guilty party but scolding the workgroup as a whole. Individual workers know who the culprit is when the boss complains, but they absorb the dehumanizing toxin and become less human in the process.

The Opposite of Support

A classic toxin is the "sink-or-swim" attitude for people new in a job. Why is it that people who are good at one job are promoted and expected to perform with little or no support? The Peter Principle is a real thing and may be due to zombification. People can and want to grow. They do not want to wither and die in a desolate environment, and they do not want to drown in a sea of uncertainty and incomprehensible demands. Where there is not adequate support, there is death, slow and painful, but ironically including a regular life-continuing paycheck.

Secrets / Employee Disengagement

Secrets are a toxin that employees bring upon themselves (with management as complicit accomplices). Employees will always complain among themselves. They won't share these moans and groans with management, preferring to massage the irritant like tonguing a loose tooth. The problem arises and the toxin takes effect when the secrets are important and solvable problems. Employees who share these concerns only with other employees are saying to management, "If you don't care, we don't care." This attitude dehumanizes everyone.

Zombie Accounting

Executives and middle management are the prime source of dehumanizing toxins. They are the ones who design business structures that focus on profit one hundred times more than people. "Of course we do," they will say. "As we learned in business school, profit is the reason for business." That would be fair enough if the profit calculation included the human costs of doing business. Subtract zombification as a cost of focusing on profit, however, and most businesses would be failures. Few see or understand this. Thus, the larger the business, the more likely it has become a zombie company.

Companies spend significant amounts of money and time to ensure that their production activities do not run afoul of environmental regulation—or else risk incurring significant financial penalties for polluting the environment. That's great, but what's the corollary to prevent the mistreatment of employees when study after study reveals the epidemic of real physical and psychological damage inflicted on workers from the workplace?

Large organizations, for example, can lop off ten percent of the workforce during down times without flinching, as blithely as a zombie losing an arm. Even without a financial crisis, large companies seem to operate from the principle that we're so big, a few zombies here and there won't make a significant difference. It makes a difference, of course, but few leaders understand the extent of the zombie problem. Norman Bodek, a practical man and the "godfather of Lean" in the United States, asks this question: Why is inventory measured and reported down to the penny, but an organization's most important asset, the knowledge and creativity of people, is nowhere on a balance sheet? The underutilization of people is one of Lean Thinking's forms of waste, but where is it measured?

What are the top five metrics for your company's health? Unless at least one is about employee well-being, you may be part of a zombie organization. Are human factors anywhere on the balance sheet? If not, you probably are part of a zombie organization. When Bodek speaks at conferences, he often asks the audience what their favorite day of the week is. The answer is always Friday. "But where do you spend most of your life?" he asks. "At work, of course, then why isn't Monday, Tuesday or Wednesday your favorite day? I believe our superiors have just not inspired and motivated us to want to come, joyously, to work." Zombies don't feel joy.

Zombie organizations drain the lifeblood from employees. It is beyond the scope of this chapter and this book to list the probable thousands of toxins that exist in the workplace. What we can do is share how to eradicate the worst of them.

Zombie-Proof Your Company

Zombies are dead. You must foster a workplace that enriches living human beings. Life must flourish in all corners. You do not have to create life, just support it.

Life is full of possibilities. Life is distinguished by having metabolism: the intake of fuel converted to the energy necessary to take on the challenges of life. Life is full of passion and possibilities. E. B. White may have described it best.

> At eight of a hot morning, the cicada speaks his first piece. He says of the world: heat. At eleven of the same day, still singing, he has not changed his note but has enlarged his theme. He says of the morning: love. In the sultry middle of the afternoon, when the sadness of love and of heat has shaken him, his symphonic soul goes into the great movement and he says: death. But the thing isn't over. After supper he weaves heat, love, death into a final stanza, subtler and less brassy than the others. He has one last heroic monosyllable at his command. Life, he says, reminiscing. Life.

Alive things respond to others and the environment, always trying to avoid negative outcomes and advance the positive. Alive things grow, reproduce, learn, and evolve. Advanced living things change their environments, communicate, create purpose, and mourn loss. Alive things are vital, and have vital signs. By contrast, when lack of support causes zombification of one employee, other employees feel the sting and are infected one after the other.

The Greeks, one of the first civilizations to try to understand life, explored different ways of doing so, including medicine, government, and philosophy. They also took a look at love, defining four types: *storge*, affection; *eros*, sexual love; *philia*, brotherly love; and *agape*, seeking the other's highest good. Agape love is about as far from zombie life as possible.

Which raises the question: On the continuum from zombie to agape, where is your company? Where should your company be? We think *agape* love for your employees should be a driver of your business. Employees working forty hours a week spend about half of their awake time working and commuting. That time should bring joy and fulfillment. Recent research by HealthStream, Inc., shows "companies that effectively appreciate employee value enjoy a return on equity and assets more than *triple* that experienced by firms that don't. When looking at *Fortune*'s '100 Best Companies to Work For,' stock prices rose an average of fourteen percent per year from 1998-2005, compared to six percent for the overall market." Morality makes money.

What has to happen is straightforward. Leaders must promote organizations that are life fulfilling and not zombie producing. Workers should be empowered and encouraged to innovate and succeed at creating and delivering goods and services that delight the customer. The role of the manager must be to help workers to unlock this potential to work together and to guard against bloodsucking bureaucracy and internal distractions. Employees have to feel valued, and optimally, feel joy in the workplace.

The secret is flow. Stagnant ponds lie still while living streams flow. Movement must happen every day for all employees. A classic example of flow is a company's vision statement. A vision is the promise of a greater tomorrow. If a company does not have a vision, or the vision is uninspired, employees have only day-to-day drudgery to endure for that paycheck. Heads are down, doing the same work every week, every month, every year. There is no movement. There is no promise of a better tomorrow to engage them or pull them forward. Work just consists of finishing an endless series of tasks. There is no grand design. There is only climbing out of the grave, stumbling after flesh, and returning to the grave.

Another sign of flow is innovation. Innovation is created by people who are interested and feel the urge to contribute. Innovation is creating something out of nothing by people who want to improve things in every way that works. Toyota claims that twenty percent of its profits are due to money-saving ideas from employees.

Management stops flow by impeding movement. Undead employees focus on one outcome—pleasing the boss—and not on moving themselves and the business forward. It is difficult to design a workplace that encourages joy in the work. However, ponder the difference between employees who are told what to do and those who are encouraged to contribute from their point of view. Management by results would seem to encourage flow, but it encourages only one measure of success; movement in a rut is zombie movement.

Flow makes work exciting. In a Lean environment, quick-flowing production requires nimble workers who find ways to improve production; thinking at work is a necessity because of ever-changing conditions; this is flow. Employees are learning and adapting all the time; this is flow too.

To love your job is flow. There is the urge to contribute, to improve, to ensure the best work is done and the greatest product is created.

Flow is ensuring that tomorrow differs from today—not necessarily better, but different, because some of the most impactful improvements are not arrived at incrementally but through learning from mistakes. Try a new way of getting the work done, especially if suggested by those doing the work. Talk about who is doing what and how the work can be better distributed. Talk about making next week better than this week and how much things will change over the next six months. Flow is imagining tomorrow. To pursue new goals is flow. Make sure goals are interesting and engaging. Measuring progress is flow.

People development is flow.

Flow is moving up Abraham Maslow's hierarchy of needs:

1. Biological and Physiological needs: air, food, drink, shelter, warmth, sex, sleep, etc.
2. Safety needs: protection from elements, security, order, law, limits, stability, etc.
3. Belongingness and Love needs: work group, family, affection, relationships, etc.
4. Esteem needs: self-esteem, achievement, mastery, independence, status, dominance, prestige, managerial responsibility, etc.
5. Self-Actualization needs: realizing personal potential, self-fulfillment, seeking personal growth and peak experiences.

Teaching and mentoring others creates flow.

Define flow as anything that pulls your employees forward.

Define "forward" as a better place for them and the business.

On one hand, to become an evil entity and create a deadly organization and dead employees:

1. Measure only financial well-being and neglect frequent (daily) people measures.
2. Hire managers who do not understand the care and support of people.

3. Impede individuality and emotionality wherever you can and avoid forming teams.

By contrast, to enhance life and your business:

1. Encourage and enable dialogue and problem-solving at every level.
2. Make today a good day for people and tomorrow an even better one.
3. Foster diversity.

However, we think you should take it a large step forward and enhance what are called the Seven People Assets™. They are:

1. Teamwork
2. Leadership
3. Communication
4. Problem-solving
5. Engagement
6. Reward
7. Knowledge

Every employee working on these areas creates the right flow in the right direction. Whatever you do, do something; the more employees you have, the more likely you are zombifying them.

Survival Guide

Determine your level of zombification by placing an X in the appropriate block, and then count the number of Xs per column.

7 People Assets	Disagree	Mixed	Agree
Teamwork • Our organization works well in teams instead of "every person for themselves." • Our culture is one of "we," not internal "us vs. them" struggles.			
Leadership • When mistakes happen, the first question is "why?" not "who?" • Employees perceive managers as supportive and enablers of value vs. degrading and generators of bureaucracy.			
Communication • Information flow is transparent throughout the organization.			

• Employees feel like they understand the organization's direction.			
Problem-solving • Staff are empowered and encouraged to innovate and make decisions. • Most problems are solved by those closest to the information vs. by managers or outside experts.			
Engagement • Employees feel a sense of ownership for the organization and take initiative to improve. • Employees enjoy their work.			
Reward • Employees are recognized for their contributions. • Financial incentives are primarily shared bonuses.			
Knowledge • Employees are encouraged and supported to develop professionally. • Employees and managers freely transfer knowledge in the spirit of being a learning organization.			
COUNT Xs			

• Multiply number of "Disagree" Xs by -2 • Multiply number of "Mixed" Column by 0 • Multiply number of "Agree" Xs by 2			
Add the adjusted scores for the "Disagree" column and the "Agree" column			

Score	Next Steps
If your score is less than zero, your culture is undead.	Reread this chapter to determine ways to exorcise the poison in your organization.
If your score is between 0 and 3, your culture is at risk of zombification.	Work with employees to identify specific opportunities to improve scores in areas you marked as "Disagree."
If your score is greater than 3, either your culture is alive or you are too optimistic.	Verify with employees that your assessment is correct. If so, great job! Give yourself a pat on the back and be on guard against future zombie attacks!

Quick zombie check. Ask employees what their personal mission is at work. Zombies don't have one.

Law of Malignancies

To maintain that competition is the sole method by which superiority can be tested and established leads to the inference that competition is a thing so beneficial that, so far as possible, it should be allowed to rage unchecked. But competition is in itself largely due to artificial causes; and it is not true that the competitive spirit is the source of all progressive development, even in the natural sphere. Competition is very far indeed from always leading to upward movement…The effect of competition is to prevent any form from attaining its maximum development, and to maintain a certain comparatively low level for all forms that succeed in surviving.
-Sidney Low, *The Living Age*, vol. 263

6 | *Internal Competition Causes Cancer*

Our species glorifies competition.

We humans seem proud of our exalted status on the evolutionary ladder, owed more to our propensity for violent confrontation—as evidenced by our not-so-vestigial fingernails and fangs—than our superior minds. Our thirst for the hot, coppery taste of blood is part of our genetic code and permeates most aspects of our lives. Legions of sports fans rejoice or agonize over their favorite teams with each play. Prime time reality television pits would-be singers, actors, marksmen, antiques shoppers, mixed martial artists, and beauty pageant toddlers against each other for riches and glory. We can't get enough of someone dominating someone else.

External Competition

Competition is the critical ingredient in evolutionary advancement. It hinders the least biologically advantaged members of a species from passing their inferior genes to the next generation, which strengthens the overall ability of the species to survive and thrive. This Darwinian model applies equally to the marketplace. Organizations that are well-suited to adapt to changing conditions and who can best meet their customers' requirements at the most efficient level of production survive. They win at the expense of less efficient or effective rivals.

With the exception of unnatural friction in a marketplace (illegal activities or prejudicial government intervention), survivors are those who internalize hard lessons from their competition and innovate to cultivate competitive advantages. From a consumer's perspective, competition is great because each company's fight for survival depends on its ability to please us while producing products cheaply enough that we can afford to buy them.

The Cancer of Internal Competition

When it comes to competition, like many things in life, there can be too much of a good thing. It's necessary to apply our competitive instincts in the marketplace to win finite wealth, market share, and customer loyalty from our rivals. The problem is that it's too easy and all-too-common for us to overextend the Darwinian competition dynamic to *within* the walls of our organization. Competition *among* organizations generates innovation and the fruits of consumer power; competition *within* organizations is a cancer that degrades collaboration and camaraderie and can destroy the organization from inside.

Any competition produces winners and losers. When applied to relationships within an organization, competition among employees leads to some workers benefitting in terms of compensation, stature, and influence at the expense of others. Unlike competition among rival companies, the irony of intra-organizational competition is that it pits people against one another who are expected to work together to promote the common competitiveness of the group. Are internal losers a necessary cost for external success?

Internal competition is not a prerequisite for employees to work hard, innovate, and be productive. Is it more than plausible that a scientist, automobile mechanic, lawyer, or accountant can contribute and grow in her craft without having to be subject to a zero-sum system of internal competition that mandates winners and losers? Is it possible to be great at what you do without having to make a loser out of someone else in the process?

In his book *No Contest: The Case Against Competition*, Alfie Kohn summarized his research into the impacts of internal competition:

> Success and competition are not at all the same thing. Competition need never enter the picture in order for skills to be mastered and displayed, goals set and met... Superior performance not only does not require competition; it usually seems to require its absence.

It seems that internal competition is encouraged for two reasons. First, internal competition is promoted to cull the herd of less desirable workers while advancing the most desirable workers to positions of relative power and influence. This is perhaps an understandable but gross misapplication of our tendency to adapt an instinctive alpha pack mentality to organization design. Second, internal competition can be an accidental by-product of the well-intentioned attempt to stimulate individuals to grow and stretch their own performance.

Up-or-Out

We discussed earlier how the conventional hierarchical pyramid model can lead to a host of negative consequences. One common way internal competition is applied is to force employees through a funnel-shaped series of promotion filters that gradually winnows talented people as the available number of privileged positions shrinks to just one ultimate leader. What can emerge is an up-or-out model, in which there is a single desirable career trajectory predicated on exemplification of a predefined set of executive attributes. Employees who are deemed by established leadership to demonstrate these attributes more than their peers rise in title and privilege; those who do not, regardless of their other contributions or demonstration of other useful capabilities, may be pushed aside or even processed out.

This up-or-out dynamic, whether a stated corporate value or an implicit model, pits workers against their peers in a beauty contest. Managers at higher tiers decide, based on their individual perceptions and political agendas, who should succeed and thrive and who should be pushed aside or pushed out.

Note that the established set of up-or-out attributes only comprises one of many organizational archetypes—the executive archetype. Many other valuable archetypes needed for the survival of the organization, like subject matter experts, innovators, coaches, etc., are less valued. At the extreme, some attributes that can be handy in an up-or-out culture can even be counter to the interests of a healthy organization. How much customer value is there in self-promotion, politicking, and kissing up? A 2005 survey of Fortune 500 CEOs showed that ninety percent are above average height, and thirty percent were at least six feet two inches tall compared to less than four percent of the overall United States population. A Duke University study suggests that "CEOs also often require thick eyebrows, a solid jaw line and small, piercing eyes." These statistical anomalies might make sense if we were recruiting for basketball teams or actors for television commercials; it's absurd when we consider that irrelevant characteristics like appearance can define how much influence, authority, and compensation employees have.

In an article titled "The myth of the visionary leader," *The Boston Globe* observed:

> Researchers who study leadership—and there are many—are beginning to offer up a surprising truth: The kind of leaders we idolize may be the last people we really want in charge. The character traits that tend to convince us someone deserves power, these thinkers say, have remarkably little to do with how effective that person will be at actually running a city, or a company, or a nation.

In other words, attributes often associated with executives like charisma, boldness, and assertiveness may be less useful to effective organizational leadership than the ability to unleash the potential of employees, the ability to identify and take quick advantage of market opportunities, and the ability to motivate people to work well as a team.

It's impossible to estimate what the cost must be to organizations and to the economy overall. Tally up the casualties of up-or-out systems, including demoralized workers and the opportunity cost of talented and otherwise motivated and loyal employees who are cast aside because they don't fit some predetermined mold. It's a ridiculous but all-too-true cliché that the more capable employee who is a quiet, dedicated team player is likely to be passed over for the extroverted self-promoter.

Performance Appraisals and Forced Curves

To be sustained over time, hierarchies require a continual succession plan to replenish leaders who leave, voluntarily or otherwise. Since each higher tier in the pyramid contains fewer people, advancements require ever more intense competition among peers to secure increasingly desirable and scarcer senior roles. A common way to push employees through the up-or-out filter is the standard performance review. Performance reviews assess the viability of each worker according to a formal, choreographed approach, generally once or twice per year. What is more, performance evaluations may include a forced curve or stack rank performance appraisal system. To improve the corporate gene pool, organizations force-fit employees into a basic bell curve type model. Common HR practice suggests that internal competition models like forced curves serve four primary functions:

- First, performance appraisal models are meant to channel feedback from managers to workers about the strengths and weaknesses of their performance. Feedback is accompanied with advice as to how the employee can improve his performance to one day potentially be promoted into a more senior role.
- Second, performance appraisal systems help to prune out employees who are deemed to be below a baseline of acceptable performance.

- Third, performance reviews elevate the station, and thereby the influence and resources, of individuals who are judged to exemplify predefined ideal attributes of the organization. A forced performance curve is a closed system in which a chosen few can succeed and thrive at the expense of others who, on paper, share the same organizational goals and purpose as the elite.
- Fourth and finally, performance reviews are a legalistic shield to document signed evidence of a worker's shortcomings to justify unfortunate treatment, such as being passed over for promotions, desired roles, and awards, and for lower compensation and even termination.

Zero-Sum Game

Forced distributions of performance evaluations create a zero-sum condition. People succeed or fail based on their relative performance against their peers, as opposed to an absolute assessment of their actual individual performance. In this model, it is more advantageous to work at an average level of performance and effort on a team with poor performers than to exert above average effort and capability on a team of exceptional peers.

Forced performance curves can be a convenient tool of manipulation by some leaders to introduce additional friction into an organization in order to accommodate competing agendas. People in positions of influence can abuse their station by violating the integrity of performance models to promote friends or lackeys.

Promotions, awards, and performance models are also filtered by the requirement to meet various political quotas.

The more friction (as opposed to flow) there is, the more a sense of have-versus-have-not is induced, with all of its accompanying destructive externalities.

This reminds us of the adage that when a group of people is being charged by a bear, it isn't necessary to be faster than the bear; you just need to be faster than the slowest person. Of course, this dynamic is counter to the stated purpose of a forced curve, which is to advance the most talented workers while pushing out the worst performers. As W. Edwards Deming described it, when these kinds of performance ratings are used, "Everyone propels himself forward, or tries to, for his own good, on his own life preserver. The organization is the loser."

Consider the example of Enron's infamous performance review system, as noted by C. William Thomas in the Journal of Accountancy (March 31, 2002):

> As Enron's reputation with the outside world grew, the internal culture apparently began to take a darker tone. [CEO Jeffrey] Skilling instituted the performance review committee (PRC), which became known as the harshest employee-ranking system in the country. It was known as the "360-degree review" based on Enron values: respect, integrity, communication and excellence (RICE). However, associates came to feel that the only real performance measure was the amount of profits they could produce. In order to achieve top ratings, everyone in the organization became instantly motivated to "do deals" and post earnings. Employees were regularly rated on a scale of 1 to 5, with 5s usually being fired within six months. The lower

an employee's PRC score, the closer he or she got to Skilling, and the higher the score, the closer he or she got to being shown the door. Skilling's division was known for replacing up to fifteen percent of its workforce every year. Fierce internal competition prevailed and immediate gratification was prized above long-term potential. Paranoia flourished and trading contracts began to contain highly restrictive confidentiality clauses. Secrecy became the order of the day for many of the company's trading contracts, as well as its disclosures.

How well did that system turn out?

Accuracy and Fairness

How accurately can relative performance be measured? Organizations with formal performance review systems try to convince their employees about how fair the system is to preempt legitimate concerns about mistreatment resulting from the approach. To be a fair system, three factors would need to be present.

First, managers would have to have perfect knowledge about their workers' performance. They would need to understand how much of an employee's perceived accomplishments were legitimate as opposed to exaggerated claims, taking credit for others' work, or inefficiencies hidden from the manager. In reality, leaders don't have a complete picture of what their employees do. Many are unable or unwilling to invest the time to understand. Even where worker output can be measured, such as sales revenues or widgets produced, enterprising employees can find ways to position their performance to achieve more favorable appraisals.

Second, a truly fair comparative assessment requires that the evaluated workers conduct the same work, with the same level of difficulty, risk of failure, and empowerment to do the job. This is often not the case. Even when the evaluated population conducts identical tasks, they may be exposed to inconsistent external factors outside their control that could influence performance. Unpredictable working conditions by shift teams or upstream suppliers or different levels of support and mentorship by different supervisors create variation. As a result, performance curves will yield an apples-to-oranges dynamic among employees in the same evaluation grouping.

Third and finally, fair assessments require the evaluator to be immune to subjective influence. Some managers make, at most, a feeble pretense at objectivity when supporting workers they favor. Even conscientious managers are still human and subject to the personal bias of workers based on perceived favorable affinities or negative preconceptions.

No performance appraisal event is perfect, and few are anywhere near that mark. Considering that compensation, station, and job security are heavily influenced by performance evaluations, how much imperfection and unfairness in the system is acceptable? The answer is that performance evaluation systems, particularly forced curve-type approaches, are not fair. Fairness in canned feedback systems is largely a fiction and irrelevant.

What matters is not that a system is fair but that it actually works. The problem is most organizations' performance evaluations are ineffective and damaging, and they violate the ridiculous and unachievable notion of fairness so often hyped by management.

Induced Rivalry

Performance curves put workers in an untenable position. They must collaborate with their peers to be seen as team players, while also delivering quality performance that is at least on par with—and ideally better than—their peers. You can look good by doing a good job *or* you can look good by comparison if your peer appears to be doing a less good job.

As a result, workers have two levers they can pull: One is their own motivation and capability to perform their duties at an acceptable level; the other is their motivation and capability to position their work as being at least as good as that of their peers to present a favorable relative perception. Organizations are only concerned with the former lever. Managers believe the double-edged internal competition created by a forced curve will both encourage workers to excel and discourage workers from underperforming.

The greed to achieve the trappings that accompany superior relative performance grades and the desperation to avoid below average relative grades are powerful motivators. These encourage unintended negative behavior that is antithetical to collaboration.

At its worst, this winners and losers dynamic is reminiscent of the Marquis de Sade's assertion that "all is unceasing and rigorous competition in nature; the desire to make off with the substance of others is the foremost—the most legitimate—passion nature has bred into us." De Sade's assessment seems to fit the corporate reality.

Manufactured Competition

Channeling the natural competitive impulse to fix problems or discover new opportunities can be an effective and often fun way to focus a team's creative energy. One technique that works well is to sponsor periodic "bake-offs," in which multiple teams comprised of employees from different functions are formed for half a day. Each team is assigned the same challenge to resolve a specific problem or to develop an innovative concept. Each team presents its idea to a panel of employees and leaders at the end of the session, and the winning team receives a token recognition, perhaps a gift certificate. Like a game, this type of competition brings people across the enterprise together constructively, builds the competency of team problem-solving and advances the organization's interests.

Unfortunately, in our experience, competition is more often used as an internal wedge than a unifying approach. A particularly insidious practice we occasionally observe is for leaders to manufacture competition between peer groups or middle managers who are perceived to be up-and-coming. In the 1920s, Alfred Sloan intentionally assigned overlapping responsibilities among different divisions at General Motors to induce a rivalry in which one division would outperform the others through some combination of innovation, efficiency, and political scheming. Imagine how GM would have benefited if this competitive energy were aimed at the real competition!

This same approach is more common than you might think. Multiple product groups or brand teams are assigned to develop the same new product concept. Peer departments are deliberately starved of sufficient budget and staffing to meet their requirements. This provokes a sort of life-and-death struggle in which the winning group earns the privilege to exist for another year at the expense of the rival. The losing groups are typically stripped down or reorganized out of existence.

Individual Incentive Programs

Another popular technique used to fan the flames of internal competition is to create an incentive system that celebrates individual achievement, as opposed to promotion of the common good of the organization.

The rationale for individual incentive programs is to push workers to contribute more than they normally would. Workers will work harder on activities that promote the interests of the company if offered incentives of financial compensation or stature. Since all workers understand that resources set aside to support incentive programs are finite, workers vie against one another to be the one to win the prize.

This is not to say that recognition of workers is destructive. It's nice to be acknowledged for achieving a personal goal or for using our unique skills to advance the greater good of the organization. Used in the right way, some individual recognition can be a powerful incentive to drive future breakthrough activity.

A culture that emphasizes individual recognition over team recognition, however, signals that, rather than being a unified group, the organization is actually a loose federation of separate entities. The group may interact for common purpose, but it succeeds or fails based on the achievements of each individual. Individual recognition becomes damaging when it motivates employees to prioritize what they can do separately to maximize personal gain rather than how they can collaborate with others to maximize organizational success. Well-structured incentive programs encourage people to put in extra effort that should benefit the greater good of the organization; the difference is that shared incentives encourage individuals to harness the collective potential of a team. An African proverb states, "If you want to go fast, go alone; if you want to go far, go together." With the extreme exception of moments of personal genius innovation, short isolated bursts of individual achievement rarely advance the interest of the overall organization in an impactful way. In business, sustainable gains that help the business to go far are almost always to be prioritized because their advantage can be leveraged widely and institutionalized—the 1+1=3 synergy effect.

In addition, work cultures that emphasize individual incentives risk destroying teamwork and camaraderie. In a team in which awards are unevenly distributed, creating stars and also-rans, the team is not really a team at all. Shared incentives promote *esprit de corps*, while individual incentives promote *esprit de singularis*. Nothing will rip a team apart faster than the negative impacts that often come with individual recognition. Even if an individual award is based on legitimate accomplishment that did not come at others' expense or participation, it's natural for peers to be jealous. This is especially the case if the award is significant. Bad feelings will intensify if people believe that their contributions are overlooked, whether due to poor politicking, inconsiderate sponsorship by management, negative favoritism, or plain bad luck. While this petty side of human nature is regrettable, it is a reality of people working together toward common goals. It's even worse when one member of a team is singled out to receive credit for an accomplishment that others feel like they had a hand in bringing about. The overlooked teammates will justifiably feel like they've had something stolen from them and may exact retribution on or ostracize the awardee. Consider how the common scenario of a manager being rewarded for the hard work of her team results in an *us* against *them* dynamic of the workers versus the manager.

Individual Commitment-Setting

The act of setting goals is often a precursor to success, whether in business or our personal lives. Goals help us define the parameters of a desired target and inform the roadmap to achieve these objectives. In some organizations, however, the act of setting goals can be twisted into a means of instigating internal competition among employees through a process of individual commitment setting. An individual commitments approach essentially requires employees to sign a contract each year. The commitments outline what their activities and accomplishments will be and how the manager will gauge successful performance. Each set of commitments should cascade through the organization, so that managers' commitments are distributed among their direct reports.

Individual goal-setting can be beneficial. The challenge with a formal approach to setting individual commitments is that it may result in a collection of separate agendas pursued to accomplish personal goals at the expense of collaboration.

In an individual commitments culture, each person is forced to achieve his goals despite others trying to achieve their goals. As a result, workers will want to collaborate only when such cooperation furthers their own individual commitments. This can actually create a disincentive to work together if others' commitments do not align directly with our own. The time and resources we would spend helping others would become an opportunity cost that could impede our personal efforts. This impact is exacerbated when employees are evaluated on a forced curve or stack rank evaluation model. How does it benefit me to help you when you're my main competition?

The Consequences of Internal Competition

If internal competition is the prevalent state of most organizations, what is the price that companies pay for it?

Credibility Degradation

Internal competition degrades the credibility of the organization. Consider that the fundamental cause of stress is a misalignment of expectations. On the one hand, as well-meaning primates, we are conditioned to want to uphold our instinctive desire to advance the interests of our tribe against rival organizations. As a result, organizations espouse virtues like teamwork and collaboration to reinforce the reciprocal expectation that all workers are obliged to support the needs of the organization. In return, the organization and our fellow workers will treat us with fairness and consideration.

On the other hand, employees are told that to prosper—or even to remain employed—their performance must be at least on par with their peers. By asking workers to compete against the same people they are required to collaborate with, organizations send a contradictory signal. This inconsistency erodes the credibility of any platitudes about management's concern for the value and well-being of employees.

Pygmalion Effect

The binary nature of internal competition that produces winners and losers will compound the polarizing effect of what has been called the Pygmalion Effect: the self-fulfilling prophecy of performance, positive or negative, that people experience based on the perception and expectations of others in authority.

If an employee is told repeatedly that she is a strong performer through favorable stack rankings, performance grades, rewards, and titles, these positive signals will reinforce her confidence in her ability to succeed. This is great news for the privileged outliers at the positive end of the competition bell curve.

The problem with internal competition, however, is that the negative corollary to the Pygmalion Effect is also at work. Those who are deemed to be the losers in internal competition receive signals that may have a corrosive effect on morale, motivation, and self-confidence. Even workers with a distinguished track record can have their self-confidence and morale shattered by a single lower ranking or by being passed over for individual recognition.

Deming believed that unfair negative performance appraisals can lead to workers feeling "bitter, crushed, bruised, battered, desolate, despondent, dejected, inferior, some even depressed, unfit for work for weeks after receipt of the rating, unable to comprehend why they are inferior." This negative side of the Pygmalion Effect can even be manifested in workers who find themselves in the middle, fat part of the performance curve. To receive consistent signals that one is average does not inspire confidence in one's abilities or chances to excel.

It's worth mentioning that sometimes employees simply aren't a good fit for their roles for whatever reason. Sometimes hard feedback is necessary to get someone's attention. The destructive impact of the Pygmalion Effect occurs when otherwise capable and dedicated employees receive denigrating feedback because they don't stack up compared to others.

Health Concerns

Internal competition induces unnecessary personal stress on the members of the organization. Competition arouses biological impulses that are ingrained to give us every advantage to succeed in a conflict. Whether we are in a knife fight or playing checkers with our neighbor, competition can enhance our alertness, ability to focus, and energy level—but at a cost.

The binary outcome of winners and losers is helpful in our quest to win games or win in the marketplace; however, the winner-or-loser outcome becomes quite personal when our professional reputation, self-esteem, and livelihood are at stake when we are pitted against peers who ostensibly share our goals.

Given the important role that work plays in our lives, both in terms of providing material support and in terms of our egos, internal competition can generate significant stress. It is no wonder that the negative dynamics induced by internal competition at work are a critical contributor to overall workplace stress.

Research tells us that the health toll of workplace stress can be significant or even fatal, ranging from anxiety and high blood pressure to ulcers, depression, and heart attacks.

Stress can weaken the body's immune system, exposing people to colds and other illnesses. It's estimated that sixty percent of lost workdays each year can be attributed to stress. As much as seventy-five to ninety percent of visits to health care providers include stress-related factors. Stress-related health care expenses impose a huge cost on employers.

The BBC reported a study that found that "long-term stress is worse for the heart than putting on forty pounds or aging thirty years because workers deal with stress by smoking, drinking and slobbing out. Those who suffer stress for at least half their working lives are twenty-five percent more likely to suffer a fatal heart attack and have a fifty percent greater chance of dying from a stroke."

Workplace Violence

Besides health problems, workplace stressors like internal competition can also lead to workplace violence. The US Justice Department estimates that more than a million people are the victims of violence at work each year. This is about fifteen percent of all violent crime in the country. Violence in the workplace is rampant and sometimes lethal. Less violent and more numerous are attacks on cab drivers, health care employees, convenience store clerks, workers in government offices, and police officers, among others.

Aggressive behavior in the workplace ranges from common forms of passive aggression, like withholding information or not showing up at meetings, to the rarer but deadly physical assaults. Even though most aggression at work is minor, over time this can lead to significant harm, including emotional distress and diminished productivity.

Demotivation

The more we compete with our colleagues, the less energy, motivation, time, and focus we have to fight our true rivals in the market. Corporations invest massively in HR, Legal, and IT specialists to run complex bureaucracies and infrastructures dedicated to performance appraisals, rewards, and promotions. Much of the investment goes to manage the inevitable employee backlash, unplanned attrition, and lawsuits that these systems invite. *The Wall Street Journal* reported that "one third of people surveyed considered quitting their jobs because of stress and fourteen percent actually did."

Chronic diseases and even life-threatening physical and psychological conditions are brought about by the stress of internal competition. Workplace violence and abuse are spurred by employees disgruntled with their treatment. Loss of organizational credibility and trust accumulates. Massive expenditures to create, manage, and defend a serpentine infrastructure are dedicated to promoting internal competition. All of it is avoidable.

How much competitive advantage could an organization realize if it tapped into even a small percentage of this huge amount of wasted potential of both human and financial capital?

Why Does Internal Competition Persist?

If internal competition is the source of so many destructive consequences, why is it such a pervasive component of our daily working lives?

Primal Wiring

As primates, we are already wired to compete with one another in societies that promote alphas from within the ranks, who rise at the expense of others. No matter how destructive internal competition might be, it's our instinctive state. The logic is pure Darwinism: for an organization to thrive in a savage market, we must attract, retain, and promote the most capable savages at all levels, even if that means leaving a long trail of casualties in our wake. "Business is business," we say. "You have to break a few eggs to make an omelet."

Of course, the logic of internal competition breaks down when we realize that it is a misapplication of the healthy focus on competition among rivals gone too far. In the market, competition among rival organizations makes the market stronger, like two rival sprinters pushing each other to break a world record; within an organization, competition is senseless and unproductive, like arm wrestling oneself. In a body, we have a name for this kind of internally generated competition—cancer. With cancer, the body attacks itself in a misguided effort to increase internal productivity, making itself more vulnerable to external attacks from actual threats.

Inertia

Inertia is also a major contributor to the prevalence of internal competition. The classic hierarchical pyramid and accompanying internal competition drivers have remained intact since at least the Industrial Revolution, making it the default way of working in business. To be an employee means to compete with one's peers at least as much as one competes with rival organizations.

Despite many negative consequences, internal competition has flourished for generations because *it has always been this way*. As a result, internal competition is so familiar and institutionalized that it would be difficult for many of us to consider an organizational culture without it. Many of us lack the imagination or energy to look for alternatives. Even if someone took a stand against the abuses inherent in internal competition, she would risk a difficult swim against the current that would be at best frustrating and at worst occupationally terminal.

Misguided Understanding of Accountability

Internal competition is encouraged by some misguided organizations because they believe it is a necessary condition to hold employees accountable to a desired standard of performance. With its built-in incentives for winners and consequences for losers, internal competition might appear to embody both the proverbial carrot and stick to keep employees on track. Neither is necessary for individual employee accountability.

According to co-author Brown (*Earn Their Loyalty*, 2011), the three necessary conditions for personal accountability to exist in an organization are:

1. Intrinsic motivation
2. Clear goals
3. Being part of a team

There is no need for internal competition to foster accountability.

The mechanisms used to promote internal competition are patronizing forms of behavioral manipulation that appeal to the basest levels of human nature, like greed, vanity, fear, and jealousy. Internal competition is demotivating. It clouds the ability of workers to set clear goals and receive feedback about their progress in achieving those goals. It creates disincentives for teams to form. As a result, it can be argued that internal competition erodes accountability. Internal competition is more about being better than your peer than being better than the common rival of your organization.

Lack of internal competition does not preclude an organization from demanding high quality and holding all employees to the highest level of accountability. Collaborative organizations understand that most people respond much better to appeals to the highest elements of human nature: hope, generosity, teamwork, compassion, and camaraderie. As a result, organizations that eschew internal competition still own and safeguard high expectations and standards of performance and behavior.

Workers unwilling to conform to the values of a collaborative organization are pushed out to protect the culture from the harmful influence of bad apples. Fortunately, such drastic measures are seldom needed in collaborative organizations due to restrictive hiring practices that filter candidates for fit. Furthermore, in cooperative organizations, it is rare for employees to be pushed out due to inability to perform required activities. As we will discuss next, a cultural tenet of collaborative organizations is to cultivate the capabilities of willing workers through training, mentorship, encouragement, and opportunities. Nobody is good at everything, but everyone is good at something. The goal of a collaborative organization is to work together to find the proper fit for all people to contribute.

Political Manipulation

At its worst, internal competition exists because it is a tool by which a privileged faction within highly political organizations preserves its hold on status, influence, and resources. To remain in power, it is in a leader's interest to surround himself with loyal supporters whose primary concern is to protect the station of their boss. At the same time, it is not unusual for people in positions of power and resources to have rivals who desire to supplant them. In both cases, the various forms of internal competition become easy levers for leaders to manipulate in order to shield themselves with dependent minions while punishing suspected rivals.

Internal competition techniques like individual incentives, performance curves, and induced rivalries enable leaders to influence the career trajectories of favored and distrusted employees alike, under the pretense that healthy tension promotes the good of the organization. The internal competition encouraged by leaders to prop up their political ambitions is in diametrical opposition to the tenets of a healthy, collaborative organization that maximizes its collective potential against its real rivals in the marketplace.

Survival Guide

1. Identify examples of internal competition at work in your organization.
   a. What impact do these internal competitions have on the morale and collaboration of the organization?
   b. Is there an opportunity to repurpose these into more constructive, collaborative activities?
2. Identify at least three opportunities to promote healthy competition. Examples may include establishing innovation "bake-offs," as described in this chapter, or creating team recognitions or goals.

Law of Good Health

Strip away all the assumptions about what competition is supposed to do, all the claims in its behalf that we accept and repeat reflexively. What you have left is the essence of the concept: mutually exclusive goal attainment (MEGA). One person succeeds only if another does not. From this uncluttered perspective, it seems clear right away that something is drastically wrong with such an arrangement. How can we do our best when we are spending our energies trying to make others lose— and fearing that they will make us lose?
-Alfie Kohn, *No Contest: The Case Against Competition*

7 | Cooperation Cures Cancer

What would happen if organizations today were actually truthful and transparent about encouraging internal competition and how they used it? Imagine a corporation that decided one day not to hide behind HR PowerPoint slides and mercenary research to justify internal competition. This company wouldn't rationalize how forced performance curves, up-or-out career programs, individual incentive programs, etc., promoted the financial interest of the shareholders, the competitive interest of the business, and the fairness and career support for employees. Instead, what if a refreshingly honest corporation acknowledged that it is their stated intention to stoke internal competition to create a high-stakes and stressful environment that forces workers to place their livelihoods, self-esteem, and health on the line to drive a perception that they are better-than-average relative to their peers?

This organization would elevate internal competition as great theater, a bureaucratic adrenaline rush, or advanced reality television. Annual performance appraisals and individual reward reviews would be public spectacles, showcasing employees in an administrative gladiatorial conference room to the delight of cheering managers and rivals. Armed with swords and shields like self-assessments, feedback from customers, and rationalizations for failing to meet quotas, peers would face off in high-stakes battles for their careers.

Unfettered by the pretense and smoke screens that typify conventional internal competition programs, performance evaluations, competition for awards, promotion discussions, etc., would be entertaining, exciting, and honest. The spoils of victory, such as promotions, bonuses, parking spaces, offices instead of cubicles, and administrative assistants, would be distributed openly before the entire organization. Losers would be pushed to irrelevance or forced out of the organization. Both winner and loser would accept results because they would volunteer to enter the corporate *Mad Max* arena. The verdict of winner and loser would be made transparently before the organization.

If a corporation that truly celebrated internal competition existed, it would attract only those drawn to the risk to their livelihood and reputation for the opportunity to gain individual compensation and trappings of power at the expense of others. As far-fetched as this model sounds, it is the same transparent gladiator dynamic that plays out in professional athletics, entertainment, and politics. It seems that some people are drawn to this zero-sum system. There is a genuine integrity to this overtly competitive approach, even if many of us would find it distressing and intimidating to work in such an environment.

Most of the rest of us would rather feel like we are part of a healthy and collaborative team. It's more pleasant to belong to a group that works together to advance mutual long-term goals while supporting the personal goals of members. Most of us don't to want think of ourselves as people who would step on others to be successful. We don't want to look over our shoulders at peers who are also our rivals.

Curing Cancer

In business, internal competition is misguided, abusive, and destructive. The negative consequences, including the toll on mental and physical health, encouragement of workplace abuse, loss of organizational credibility and integrity, motivation loss, and decay of teamwork and accountability, far outweigh any minor gains that may be generated. Of course, the opposite of internal competition is collaboration. Given its prevalence in business culture, what can we do to help our organization replace internal rivalry with a collaborative zeal to compete against other organizations?

Deep-or-Across vs. Up-or-Out

Up-or-out organizations might give lip service to the importance of diversity in business; however, they deliberately ignore a wide range of valuable skills and capabilities in favor of one specific set of stereotypical executive qualities. The focus on diversity is limited to demographic qualities rather than a broader focus on diversity of opinions, skill sets, or creative approaches.

It would be much more effective to attract, retain, and foster a broad base of valuable and diverse skills and experience levels. Rather than penalize capable workers just because they are not deemed to show potential or interest in being executives one day, employees should be offered a *deep-or-across* system. In this model, workers have the opportunity to become experts in valuable specialties or to become generalists with exposure across different competencies.

Employees who choose the expert track will drive continual improvements in productivity and innovation in their competency, and thereby enable the organization to differentiate itself in key core competencies.

Workers who opt to be generalists will help break down functional silos through their internal networks, understanding and appreciation of other competencies, and cross-pollination of ideas across the business. From the employees' perspective, they will enjoy control over their own career paths based on personal interest.

In practice, the organization may have to place boundaries in this deep-or-across model to balance the supply of available positions with employee demand to work in specific roles. For example, this balance can be accommodated by regular and predictable job rotations for generalists and restrictive external hiring of specialists.

Effective Feedback

In our discussion of superorganisms, we highlighted the importance of the rapid and transparent flow of information to facilitate easy decision-making and decisive action. Collaborative cultures provide mechanisms for sharing valuable feedback within the organization without the negative consequences associated with performance review systems, especially forced curve systems.

In internally competitive environments, feedback is provided defensively through legalistic templates with signature lines, and feedback is received defensively through spinning of performance input and fear of perceived failure. In a collaborative environment, feedback is given and received in a direct, sincere, and well-meaning spirit of striving for continuous improvement, both personally and collectively.

Internally competitive organizations invest considerable effort in preparing formal and elaborate annual feedback events, whereas collaborative organizations strive to share feedback with one another real-time on an ongoing basis. Performance reviews in internally competitive organizations are often resented as being patronizing and irrelevant assessments pushed down by managers who are not aware enough to make credible critiques. Performance evaluations and rankings can feel accusatory and degrading when focused on what a worker has or has not done. By contrast, in collaborative organizations, feedback is sought by workers to help improve their work. Collaborative organizations use feedback to cooperatively search for the root causes of why a problem has occurred and how it can be improved to better the organization.

Note that the absence of a formal performance evaluation system does not have to preclude organizations from being able to document a necessary employee information should a pattern of employee misbehavior or performance issues need to be captured, etc.

Shared Incentives

Collaboration can be fostered through an emphasis on shared rather than individual incentives and rewards. Similar to individual focused recognition programs, shared incentives encourage employees to tap their potential and foster innovation; unlike individual incentives, however, shared incentives also promote teamwork, collaboration, and esprit de corps. Organizations are comprised of people, so there will always be a risk of human weaknesses (such as jealousy) as a by-product of any reward system; however, shared incentives help to limit negative behavioral impulses more effectively than individual recognition programs.

Depending on the organization, a moderate degree of individual recognition might be beneficial to reward workers for superlative achievement as long as proper safeguards are taken. Recognition programs need to prevent abuses like people taking credit for others' work or recognition being an undeserved gift from an insecure manager as opposed to credit for actual accomplishment.

Collaborative organizations sometimes prefer to have individual awards be nominated and selected by the employees' peers instead of by leadership. Peer-selected individual recognition can help to reduce the chance that someone receives a reward based on favoritism by management. Peer selection also helps to prevent the temptation to claim credit without properly sharing recognition, because the award requires an implicit filter that the achievement was genuine and not at the expense of peers.

Advocates of internal competition might argue that shared incentives promote a free rider problem. The free rider risk is that some recipients of group awards will benefit without working as productively as others on the team. While free riders are a real risk, collaborative cultures police this bad behavior through the social sanction of people who do not pull their weight. As a result, individuals who tend toward free rider characteristics are anomalies in collaborative organizations and are likely to be pushed out, voluntarily or otherwise.

Even where risks like the free rider problem exist in shared incentive programs, these consequences tend to be lesser evils than the destructive results of a culture that encourages individual achievement.

Shared Goals

A system of individual commitments can drive divisive behavior. In an individual commitment program, employees carry the full burden of risk of failure to accomplish a slate of objectives alone. It is a case of every person for herself. Any needed help that might be offered from others will result from coincidental overlap of goals, calculated barter of time and resources, or a rare act of charity.

By contrast, promoting goal-setting through shared objectives will have the dual benefit of tapping employee potential while also promoting teamwork and collaboration. When a team shares commitments, they also share the burden of risk of failure. Collaboration is not only enabled, it is also a necessary condition for success. As a result, shared commitments create the foundation for the multiplier effect of cooperation. In addition, the act of working together toward a common stretch goal and for a common purpose is a key success factor in establishing a sense of community. While individual commitments encourage workers to take a myopic view of their activities, team goals require employees to consider a broader context for how their efforts impact the entire organization.

Vigilance in a Collaborative Culture

There are people who are so driven to be competitive that they will never succeed in a culture that values collaboration and teamwork over internal rivalry. While it's possible for some selfish people to adapt to a collaborative environment, organizations that emphasize teamwork must be disciplined about recruiting and hiring candidates who embrace cooperation. Organizations grounded in collaboration should be selective in their recruiting process to screen for fit. They understand that a culture of teamwork can be a significant competitive differentiator; however, this culture is an asset that can be destroyed in short order if the temptation to adopt internal competition seeps in. What's more, people who work in a collaborative organization must work to safeguard the culture against the decaying effects of internal competition. All it takes is a single leader to foment a haves-and-have-nots environment by creating barriers to team identity to destroy a collaborative culture. The introduction of new titles, individual recognition programs, and peer stack rankings will expose the dark side of human nature. This may poison the organization by fostering jealousy, vanity, and greed.

Positive Pygmalion Effect

We discussed earlier how internal competition can reinforce negative messages to employees through the Pygmalion Effect. Fortunately, a collaborative culture that avoids internal competition can enjoy the positive potential of the Pygmalion Effect. Organizations that promote positive reinforcement, encouragement, optimism, and provide opportunities to grow and flourish create a constructive, self-fulfilling prophecy for employees. Employees gain confidence, motivation, and morale.

Decouple Ego from Organizational Needs

Finally, the overarching principle for any organization that wishes to be truly collaborative is collaboration requires employees to invest their egos into the needs of the organization.

Not that workers should accept insult and mistreatment. Far from it; this, after all, is how workers are expected to behave in conventional organizations. Internally competitive cultures depend fully on emphasizing and manipulating the egos of their workers as a means to control specific behavioral outcomes. Collaborative organizations replace appeals to individual egos with a focus on teamwork, objective feedback, and encouragement to drive continued personal growth and continuous improvement in the organization overall.

Cancer Cure

Competition has its place in society and serves a central role in the evolution of all creatures. Indeed, companies should do everything in their power to compete relentlessly in the daily battleground that is the marketplace. However, organizations should evolve beyond the antiquated notion that rivalry among employees, who should work together against common external threats, creates a stronger company. As Franklin D. Roosevelt noted, "Cooperation, which is the thing we must strive for today, begins where competition leaves off."

Survival Guide

What mechanisms does your organization have in place to encourage collaboration? Consider the following areas:

- Do your recruiting and hiring criteria specifically call out team-based competencies as hiring prerequisites?
- Do your hiring interviews include assessments of proven collaborative skills?
- Do your organization's values include mention of tenets related to collaboration?
- Do you know how to create and sustain teams?
- Do you have formal team-based incentives for rewards and recognition in place?
- Do you encourage team-based goals?
- If you conduct regular employee surveys, how well does your organization rate in terms of collaboration and teamwork?

Law of Boundaries

As you simplify your life, the laws of the universe
will be simpler; solitude will not be solitude, poverty
will not be poverty, nor weakness weakness.
-Henry David Thoreau, *Walden*

8 | *Amoebas Rule*

If evolutionary success is species longevity, it should not be surprising that some of the most successful creatures on earth exhibit two common characteristics: simplicity and organic cooperation.

Take the example of the amoeba. *Amoeba* comes from the Greek word for "to change," and its ability to adapt swiftly and completely to changes in its environment has helped to ensure its survival. Amoebas are simple, single-celled animals that move by changing body shape, creating false feet into which the rest of the body flows.

Simplicity

The general advantage of simplicity should be self-evident: the fewer the moving parts, the less opportunity there is for breakage. The cost of coordination is less when there are fewer parts to manage. The simpler the organism, the easier it is to establish purity of focus. Sure, an amoeba is still limited in its capabilities relative to complex multicellular creatures. That said, the lowly amoeba consists of only eight distinct parts, most of which is liquid endoplasm. Yet for billions of years, it has survived and thrived, carrying out sophisticated activities including digestion, self-propulsion, and reproduction.

As with biological organisms, simplicity is useful to the long-term success of business organizations. The less complex, the easier it is to adapt and be flexible, the fewer opportunities there are to create mistakes and the easier it is to observe errors. We weave complex webs of policies, rules, and departments because we can, only to entangle ourselves in our own sticky bureaucratic strands.

Process efficiency experts tell us that seventy to ninety percent of almost any process consists of non-value-added activity. Much of this waste is hard to see, because we are numb to it or waste is hidden under other layers of waste. The complexity we create for ourselves slows our functions, restricts our flexibility, frustrates our employees, and angers our customers, and the majority of it is unnecessary.

When we consult with clients about their operations, we ask the same question over and over: "Is this activity necessary?" The first answer is almost always yes, followed by a long-winded defense of an indefensible system. However, it usually doesn't take long to break through justifications and excuses to arrive at the truth: what matters is that the organization creates and delivers value to customers through the exertions of employees and partners. Pretty much everything else that doesn't contribute to value generation is wasteful and unnecessary. The closer an organization can get to stripping away unnecessary activity, processes, organizational artifacts, and systems to approximate the ideal amoebic simplicity, the simpler and more efficient it will be.

Responsiveness

An important design criterion of amoebas is their incredible responsiveness to their environment. Although lacking formal senses, amoebas can still detect and respond to environmental changes such as light (phototaxis) or chemicals (chemotaxis). When an amoeba detects a food source (think customers), it surrounds it, maximizing its exposed surface area around the target.

Unlike amoebas, most businesses find it challenging to understand and respond to their environments. They lack insight into their customers' needs and attitudes, and they are unaware of competitive threats from their rivals. They are not instantly responsive to requests or complaints from customers and lack the flexibility to respond to and counter competitors' actions. We find that many organizations are not even clear about who their customers are or how their customers define value.

Unlike amoebas, many organizations expose very little of their organization directly to the point of value, the customer, and instead devote much of their resources to internal operations. If amoebas dedicated as little relative resources to attacking prey as most organizations dedicate to pleasing their customers, they would starve.

Value Osmosis (Flow)

Besides exhibiting a simple structure, amoebas interact with their world through a process called osmosis. Through osmosis, the amoeba's outer skin allows water to flow through its systems via a semipermeable membrane. As opposed to more complex organisms with distinct and complicated internal systems, an amoeba's semipermeable body allows water to move throughout its system unimpeded by rigid structures. Semipermeability enables the amoeba to interact with life-giving water in a much more connected way than most other creatures whose bodies physically separate them from their environment.

Osmosis is essential to life because without it cells would dehydrate and die. In business, the value we deliver to our customers is like water in cells. If we aren't successful in providing a good or a service to our customers that at least meets their requirements, then we will go out of business. And like water permeating through the cells in our bodies, we can observe how value flows through our organization as we create and deliver the products our customers demand.

We do not have a term like osmosis to describe the flow of value through our organizations, and for good reason. In most organizations, value does not flow unencumbered through departments and teams like water passing from cell to cell. In our businesses, value is diverted around rigid functional walls and hits occasional dead ends created by policies, organizational barriers, complex or unsynchronized technology, and any other obstacle that impedes the flow of value.

A primary contributor to the lack of flow of value through the organization is overspecialization. The amoeba has but a few parts that act together to meet all the needs of the organism. In most businesses, we assign discrete functions to divisions, departments, groups, and teams. Departmental specialization enables a particular group to focus on one specific area of the business without distraction from other requirements of the organization; however, the tendency is for each organizational unit to separate itself from the rest of the business. The more rigid the separation between functions, the more difficult it is for information to circulate throughout the organization. Eventually, the business becomes more of a de facto federation of loosely aligned factions.

Note that corporate leadership is insufficient to bridge internal functional barriers to the flow of value. Most organizations pop out virtues like synergies, teamwork, and breaking down silos through internal memos, web pages, and sound bites, but internal compartmentalization of business continues to be the norm.

Managers cannot create the unimpeded flow of ideas and communication through an organization by fiat or by issuing platitudes. No amount of leadership retreats and executive coaching will soften the calcified organizational structures we build to maximize our own convenience, shield ourselves from additional work, and consolidate our political power base by amassing more resources. It is rare for a leader to willingly release her budget for employees to another division because it is the right thing to do for the business.

The silo effect within organizations caused by rigid boundaries between departments and the resulting inefficiencies is well chronicled. What we find to be less realized is how this internal compartmentalization dynamic extends to the individual employee level.

Within each organizational compartment, we assign workers into ever more specialized roles through titles and job descriptions. Organizational design tactics like performance evaluations and individual rewards are counterproductive. The corrosive impact on collaboration internal competition encourages outweighs any short-term benefits.

Organizational silos can arise when we focus more on separate business functions than on the flow of value across different functions. Silos encourage employees to think atomically (payroll, outbound marketing, shipping orders, etc.) instead of systemically. When employees limit their energies to their immediate areas of responsibility instead of taking a wider organizational perspective, their exertions will at best result in low-impact local improvements.

At worst, improvement efforts that fail to consider systemic impacts will inadvertently have a negative impact on other parts of the business. Silos promote a myopic focus that is often blind to the Law of Unintended Consequences by failing to consider ramifications to the whole system. Functional silos also lead to an opportunity cost by failing to take advantage of much more impactful cross-functional improvement activities.

Silos also contribute to a NIMBY (Not In My Back Yard) mindset. Employees whose roles are restricted to specific activities may take on an inflexible separatist perspective regarding what they will and will not do. This might range from passive resistance to the militant refusal to engage in any task not explicitly called out in their job descriptions. They lose sight of their role as contributing members to the greater good of the organization. Instead, they focus their passions on defending themselves or their teams from having to exert any additional energy on anything beyond their isolated corner of the organization. This attitude is common, maybe even pervasive.

This attitude may be observed in something as simple as the employee who steps over a piece of trash in the parking lot or fails to report a leaking faucet in the washroom. We might be tempted to dismiss this lack of ownership in the business as petty and selfish—and perhaps it is—but we should also recognize that many employees may feel separated from the organization instead of part of it, due to the reinforcing layers of silos.

The rigid partitions we build within our organizations and among our employees are not limited to blocking interaction with our fellow workers. We tend to think of our businesses as separate from the rest of the world in the same way that mankind considers itself separate from the rest of nature. It's ironic that although providing value to our customers is the reason our organization exists, we seem unable to consider dissipating the barrier that separates us from our customers.

The amoeba interacts intimately with its world through its osmotic membrane. Businesses, however, wall themselves off from their customers through impermeable barriers that limit effective interaction and impede visibility and understanding. This rigid shell around our businesses may be of a deliberate design, like when we view customers as checkbooks to be exploited through our disingenuous marketing.

Our walls may be the result of apathetic (as opposed to empathetic) interactions. We may isolate ourselves from customers through predatory fees and confusing policies. In other cases, our rigid separation from customers arises from the laziness or complacency that accompanies the false sense of security that our current market position is unassailable.

How to Fix This Problem: Flexible Amoebic Design vs. Functional Silos

Osmotic flow through semipermeable membranes should extend to our relationships with our colleagues and our customers. The ideal organizational design to capitalize on the principle of value osmosis is the Lean Thinking value stream approach.

Conventional organizational design is based on functional silos. By contrast, the value stream organization recognizes that the processes we use to create and deliver value to our customers often cut across functional lines. Our effectiveness is based on our ability to deliver what the customer wants, when they want it, and at the price they seek relative to our competition. Our efficiency is based on how well we manage resource consumption to deliver value to customers.

We discussed earlier how form must follow function. In functionally oriented organizations, we order ourselves by competency because it's convenient for us to think and manage that way. Sequester accountants, sales people, data analysts, IT specialists, and production technicians in functional islands, and force the flow of value to navigate the resulting silos. In a value stream organizational model, we reorganize ourselves to maximize effectiveness, efficiency, and clear line-of-sight to the customer as our primary design consideration—just as amoebas would.

The traditional organization will have VPs of functional specialties like HR, Finance, Operations, IT, or Sales & Marketing that cascade to smaller units of functional specialties. Value stream owners responsible for cross-functional teams aligned to customer segments lead value stream organization. A multispecialty hospital may be organized by disease type, for example, or a government agency may be organized by customer segment or category of service offered. Each value stream is staffed by the appropriate mix of functional experts who work across competencies for the common interest of the aligned customer or product.

Value stream organizations promote cross-training among employees, thus increasing capacity to be nimble and encouraging greater professional development. The cross-functional nature of value stream organizations breaks down traditional silos and increases communication and team problem-solving. Value stream orientation requires trading off some expertise from overspecialization in exchange for greater collaboration. Value stream design results in a multiplier effect of combining different expertise and the "many hands" effect of concentrating effort on addressing the customer's greatest need.

In a value stream orientation, all activities are judged by how much value they add for the customer. Internal business activities may be necessary for regulatory or administrative needs, but they do not add customer value and are minimized as much as possible. All jobs should be viewed this way—add value or change.

What matters is delivering in a differentiated way to meet customer needs and challenge competitors in a world of finite resources and customers. To manage upward only produces waste and serves no purpose. All units should work in concert, not command-and-control. Think about our biological bodies: Any siloes there? Any non-value-added activities?

The Constrained Profile vs. the Nimble (Amoebic) Profile

Constrained organizations pursue change but thwart their own efforts to implement improvements. Some intentionally avoid as much change as they can. Most see the need for some key transitions but can't execute them. Nimble (amoebic) organizations, however, succeed in unpredictable, competitive environments by quickly and creatively modifying their operations when necessary.

Symptoms of a constrained organization:

- Bewildered and discouraged behavior when faced with unanticipated problems or opportunities
- Ineffective responses when dealing with persistent disorder
- Over- or under-reaction to unfamiliar pressure
- Senior leaders seldom show a unified front around critical issues
- Slow and hesitant movement through the adaptation process, which lags behind the implementation speed of competitors
- Success evaluated on energy expended and/or what gets installed, rather than on delivery of promised results
- Bias toward being overly flexible or overly restrictive in operating style; no balance between the two
- Multiple change efforts are approached as separate endeavors; the interdependencies are overlooked
- Human, physical, technical, and financial resources take a long time to redefine and redeploy following a disruptive change
- Can absorb a single major change, but are overwhelmed when faced with multiple overlapping initiatives with significant implications

Characteristics of a nimble (amoebic) organization:

- Demonstrate a superior capacity to deal with unanticipated problems and opportunities
- Are alert, agile, and responsive when dealing with constant irregularity and disorder
- Can orchestrate multiple (overlapping or simultaneous) initiatives while maintaining productivity and quality standards
- Are led by executives who share a common understanding and sense of urgency about critical issues
- Are quick, graceful, and resourceful when adjusting to unfamiliar pressures
- Can move through the process of adapting more efficiently and effectively than the competition
- Are malleable within their existing boundaries of operation while remaining capable of redefining those boundaries, if necessary, to succeed
- Operate in a manner that balances the need for structure and discipline with creativity and flexibility
- Approach multiple change efforts with a portfolio view to ensure interdependencies are addressed
- Able to rapidly redeploy people and their physical, technical, and financial resources following a disruptive change
- Measure change success by how well promises to customers are met

Employees who work in constrained organizations have difficulty with ambiguity, identifying new opportunities, and executing well. By contrast, employees in nimble organizations embrace change, seek out new innovations, and are adept at being responsive.

Symptoms of people in constrained organizations:

- Low tolerance for ambiguity and a high need for assurances
- Tend not to engage effective problem-solving activities when faced with sustained uncertainty and ambiguity
- Become immobilized with fear and anxiety (even panic) when surrounded by turmoil
- Feel victimized by change and unable to influence their own destinies
- Feel limited by the organization's rules, policies, procedures, and power structures
- Are often preoccupied with internal struggles and struggle to focus on identifying and meeting customer needs
- Become engrossed in office politics, resource-ownership scuffles, petty bickering, and narrow-minded turf wars
- Engage in exaggerated and inappropriate conflicts
- Espouse what their boss wants to hear rather than expressing their true opinions
- Do not believe they are important to the organization's overall viability and may feel disassociated and disengaged from the individuals or groups with whom they routinely interact
- Have little enthusiasm for contributing to the operation's ultimate success except to the extent necessary to stay out of trouble or remain employed

Characteristics of people in nimble (amoebic) organizations:

- Show resilience when faced with unfamiliar and challenging circumstances

Law of Boundaries

- Expect that whatever status quo exists will soon become outdated, driving new changes into the system
- Function within flexible interpretations of their existing roles and assume that they may face new job responsibilities periodically
- Accept frequent reassignment and reordering of their priorities as the norm
- View a continuous flow of unplanned activities as the inevitable price for competing in volatile markets
- Think it is normal to deal with evolving initiatives and an abundance of diverse ideas
- Are accustomed to working in synergistic, cross-functional teams
- Refuse to be trapped by past successes or current pathologies
- Want to be involved in helping guide change projects but also expect their input will result in fast, insightful, and definitive decision-making by management
- Focus on the company's ultimate success rather than the discomforts they may experience in getting there
- Recognize and resolve or de-escalate problems quickly
- Think it is natural for employees to engage in honest dialogue, straightforward feedback, and open, constructive conflict
- Show a desire to experiment, and display a high tolerance for ambiguity
- Are multiskilled, motivated, and embrace cross-training opportunities
- Want to strengthen their identification with the company and attempt to parallel its success with their own

- Rely on their personal and team resilience attributes to accommodate the disruptions they face more quickly and effectively than the competition

The Optimal Customer Boundary (and Interior)

A cardinal rule for any organization that hopes to survive, sustain, and succeed is that customers define what has value, not the enterprise. When in doubt, think of the customer as the intended recipient of the good or service provided by the organization.

For most basic processes, we can identify who the customer is without too much trouble. The customers of the payroll process are the employees who will receive the paycheck. The customers of the grocery checkout are the purchasers of the milk and bread and ice cream. When we look at an organization at the most abstract level, however, customer identification can be difficult. Yes, our car dealership sells new automobiles to qualified buyers. But we also must consider the owner of the dealership as a customer, since she demands a certain profit level. Perhaps we would consider the employees to be customers as key stakeholders in the business whose morale and retention is critical to profitable operations.

Note that not everyone who believes he is a customer must be considered a customer. The florist next door might be perturbed by the steady flow of cars through our shared parking lot, but we aren't required to honor his requirements unless contractually obligated to do so. The federal government may exert influence over our agency due to legal and budgetary leverage, but that does not mean the feds are our customer.

Each customer has unique needs that must be respected. Our customers define what value a process, and ultimately an organization, should produce. If the goods or services we produce do not meet our end customers' standard of value, then a more responsive competitor will steal our market share. If our business does not generate the investment return to meet our shareholders' standard of value, then they may divert our funding to more appealing financial opportunities. If the way we treat our employees fails to address their standard of value relative to their compensation, they may seek better treatment elsewhere.

Our ability to meet our customers' expectation for value defines our *effectiveness* as an organization. Effectiveness indicates our customers' satisfaction with us, and is often measured in customer satisfaction and revenue metrics.

At the same time, it's not enough to generate value for our customers if we can't remain financially viable. Any activity that does not help to create value for one or more of our customer groups is wasteful.

The people, process, and technology obstacles that impede the flow of value through our organizations generate waste. Goods and services we produce that fail to meet our customers' definition of value are waste. We apply resources and energy to build reports, sit in meetings, sift through email, travel between locations, wait for approvals, edit and reedit forms. Ultimately, most things we do in a typical day are wasteful because these activities do not help to create value. Think of it this way: if you ask your customers if they will pay for an activity and they demur, then it is probably wasteful.

Even if we consistently and successfully address our customers' requirements, we will not remain in business if our costs become excessive. Our ability to generate value with the least required resource and time consumption defines our *efficiency*. Efficiency indicates how well we use our available resources, and is usually measured in some form of expense metrics. Our ability to succeed requires simultaneous management of our effective delivery of value to customers while being efficient enough to minimize wasteful expenses. This relationship is illustrated in the Value Frontier diagram below:

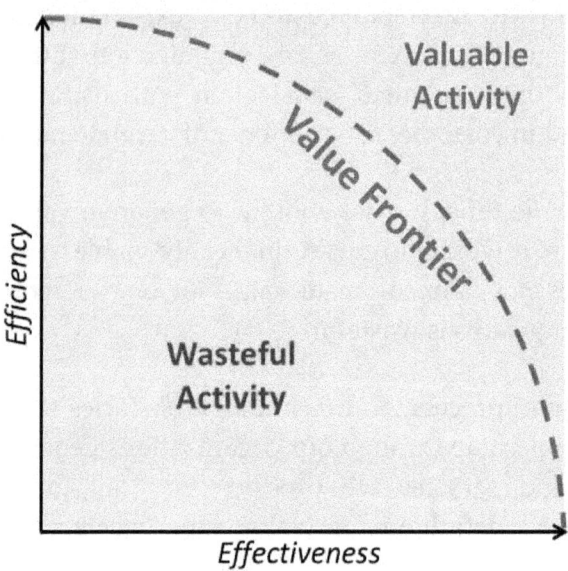

The Value Frontier captures the three elements we defined as being evolutionary differentiators of amoebas: simplicity, responsiveness, and value osmosis. Simplicity drives efficiency. Responsiveness promotes effectiveness. Value osmosis equates to maintaining a permeable connection with the customer at all times to maximize the flow of value.

Activities that are effective enough to please our customers and efficient enough for us to sustainably control costs are on the correct side of the Value Frontier. If an activity does not address the customer needs, it is wasteful and on the wrong the side of the Value Frontier. If an activity wastes resources to an unsustainable degree or is less efficient than a competitor's production process, it is also wasteful. The Value Frontier can be considered the demarcation line of profitability. If we fail to effectively deliver the results that our customers expect, no matter how efficient our processes our demand and revenue will suffer. If we consume resources excessively to meet our customers' needs, we will spend ourselves out of business. Responsible stewardship of resources requires us to deliver value with as little waste as possible. At one extreme of the Value Frontier is the Commodity point, at which the customer's requirements are simple and based on price-sensitivity. At this point, price becomes the primary differentiator in the market, so we should focus on being as efficient a producer as we can.

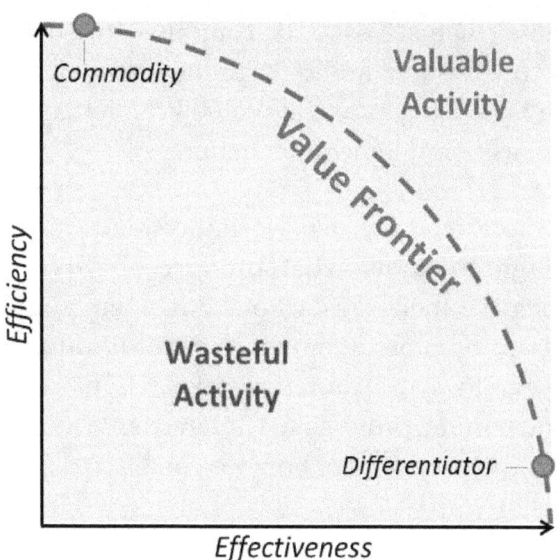

At the other extreme of the Value Frontier is the Differentiator point, at which the customer demands high quality and service, and price isn't much of a factor. At this point, the output is a luxury good, and exceptional features and service are the primary differentiators in the market. Here, we should focus on being as effective as we can, even if our production costs are high.

There is no universally right way to deliver value efficiently. The context for each organization is different. Similarly, how we address the unique demands of each of our different customer groups in a sustainable way will also differ by customer type. Our optimal business model might be to sell a lot of cheap commodities to a price-sensitive customer base, which would put us on the upper part of the Value Frontier. If our distributors enjoy a lot of leverage, they may hold us to a high burden of interaction with them, which would place them toward the bottom of the Value Frontier.

The goal of enlightened organizations that want to differentiate themselves and continue to survive is to operate processes that are as far to the upper right corner of the Value Frontier as possible. Value Frontier analysis helps to solve a basic simultaneous equation.

First, be more effective: Do we understand our customers well enough to know what product or service features would increase their satisfaction? Are there simple things we can do to be more attentive to detail in our production and delivery to avoid dumb mistakes? Can we provide a friendlier or more professional interaction with customers by being more conscious of how we come across?

Second, for those processes that create value for customers, look for opportunities to make them more efficient. Stop doing things that don't generate value for customers. Sometimes this is easy; there are usually a few low-hanging fruit opportunities we can pluck with little trouble. Should it take four people to approve that invoice? Why do you go through so much flour to produce cookies each day?

Continuous improvement in our processes helps to shift the Value Frontier down and to the left, reaching efficiency and effectiveness earlier on the continua. This shift increases the ratio of value versus wasteful activity, and ultimately increases our profitability and stability as a business.

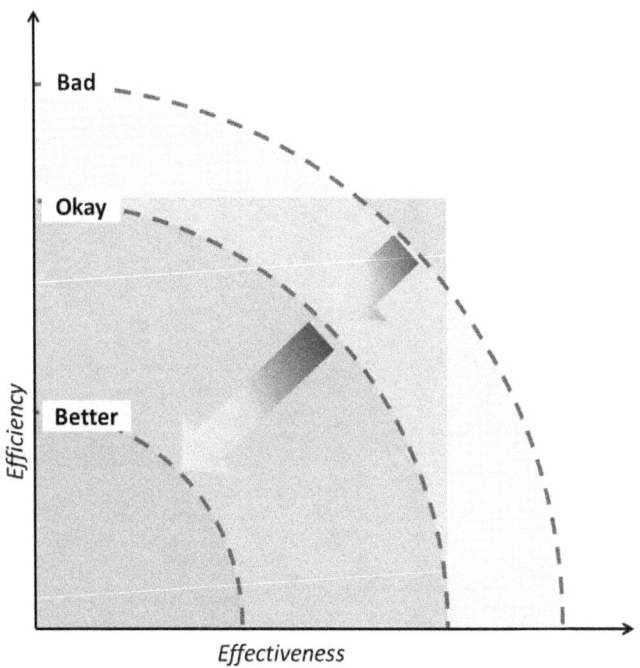

It sounds great in theory to shift the Value Frontier to maximize the amount of valuable activity we generate; however, if we assume that form should follow function, then how we design our organizations could have profound implications for our ability to unlock our hidden potential.

The Wisdom of the Amoeba

The value stream for an amoeba is simplicity personified. It maximizes physical contact with the food source, and everything is designed for the quickest and easiest intake and digestion of the food.

This is a complicated law, made complicated by jury-rigged organizational structures that we design more for internal convenience than customer contact. Amoebas understand the value stream and the concept of flow very well, certainly better than most of us. When you think about your company's survival, ask what an amoeba would do.

Survival Guide

Consider the following questions to identify opportunities for your organization to become more amoebic:

- *Simplicity*: Identify the five most inefficient processes in your organization. List out the process steps for each, and for each process step ask the following questions (in order):
  - Can we eliminate this step, task, or decision?
  - Can we combine this step, task, or decision with another?
  - Can we simplify this step, task, or decision?
  - Can we simplify or clarify the supporting policy or training for this step, task, or decision?

- *Responsiveness*: Poll your organization or team to ask the following questions. Is the answer obvious?
  - Who is your customer?
  - How do your customers define a successful engagement with your organization? How do you know?
  - How responsive is your organization or team at addressing your customers' shifting needs?
  - How could you become more responsive?

- *Value Osmosis*: Review the charts from this chapter that compare attributes of a constrained organization to a nimble (amoebic) organization.
  - How nimble is your organization?
  - What three things could you do today to become more nimble?

Law of Symbiosis

Nobody's going to fix the world for us, but working together, making use of technological innovations and human communities alike, we might just be able to fix it ourselves.
-Jamais Cascio

9 | *Survival Makes for Strange Bedfellows*

Nile crocodiles can grow to twenty feet or longer and weigh more than two thousand pounds. Their jaws can clamp on a hapless victim with a force of five thousand foot-pounds. Their natural diet includes antelope, wildebeests, hippos, giraffe, and Cape buffalo. These crocodiles are the most lethal natural predator of man, killing upward of a thousand a year. Two chomps can take off a normal-sized leg; four can rip through the middle of a more rotund target. Free from worry, however, is the plover, a bird allowed to explore the crocodile's mouth to feed on stray bits of leftover meat and ever-present leeches. This bird behavior is of benefit to both animals, preventing infection for one and providing tasty meals for the other: a good example of symbiosis.

There are many other documented instances of similar bird behavior. Egrets, for example, can ride all day on the back of large animals, picking parasites from skin and fur. More specialized is the Oxpecker, which rides on the backs of zebras doing the same thing. Microbes are the most numerous of the symbiotic species, including those in the human gut, enhancing digestion for us and providing ABC (already been chewed) tidbits for them.

There are three kinds of symbiotic interactions: mutualism, like the plover and crocodile; parasitism, which includes tapeworms, fleas, and ticks; and prey-predator, an example being free-range chickens raised by humans to slaughter. All three are important to understand organizational survival.

All organizations can have a symbiotic relationship with their customers or constituents; one provides a product or service while the other pays for or endorses it. This relationship is common, researched, and well understood… if not always done well. However, there is another more long-living symbiotic relationship than transient customer interactions, one that is much more lethal: customer reviews on the Internet.

Knowledgeable business people recognize that dissatisfied customers can be a wealth of information. In the day-to-day world, comment cards are filled out, collected, and scored, with results used to improve services at a later date. This is the worst use of customer reviews. Better is to find out in the moment if there are any problems so they can be fixed immediately and amends can be made. Studies show this action can improve customer satisfaction and loyalty.

The Internet is a Different World

On the Internet, normal business-customer symbiosis is disconnected. The customer fills out an order form and a few days later the item is dropped off on their porch. There is no "Good morning, how is your day going?" No joy at viewing the item being purchased and discussing how wonderful it is. No "Thank you" as the customer walks out the door. There are certainly prey-predator relationships, with all the Internet scams we must avoid, but that is not where our new Darwinian dangers lie. And like most dangers, we do not pay enough attention to the possibilities. And one of those possibilities is the death of your company.

Angie's List might be the most familiar Internet business review site. Touted as a place where companies cannot purchase favorable comments, customers have to buy a membership to provide and read the reviews. Companies are given letter grades, A-F, and written summaries of the customer's experience. Those reviewed can add a response. This comment-response is where symbiosis can be mutual, beneficial to both customer and business, or parasitic, where one wins at the expense of the other.

Common in this world of social media is the consumer who is dissatisfied and wants the world to know it. The old adage that a satisfied customer may tell a few others while one who is dissatisfied will tell a dozen or more is indeed old; the dissatisfied can now tell tens of thousands and do it for a long, long time.

Here is an example of an Angie's List complaint. This company received a C grade:

> Description of Work:
>
> We had A/V cabinets (lower cabinets with doors and then shelves above) built in our family room and master bedroom.
>
> Member Comments:
>
> The end product was good but the installation process was very frustrating. We had to stop the first installer because he was not planning on installing the cabinets as we had designed them. In

order to make them flush with the walls, he planned on installing a shim/spacer between the cabinets and the walls, and he told us there was nothing he could do to cover to cover up the seam that would be visible between the shim and the cabinet (like install a face plate). After emailing back and forth with the owner we learned that they could indeed install a face plate to cover the seam. That email discussion took more than a week (the owner was not particularly punctual in responding to emails). And then it took more than another week to schedule the second installer. That installer did an overall good job (and there is no seam), but only brought two shelves for the lower family room cabinet when the design was for 2 (sets of) shelves. So it took another week to get the second set of shelves. Finally, when I said the installer could use our garage for his work prepping the cabinets before bringing them in the house (it looked like it might rain) I didn't realize that meant he would be using a saw that resulted in getting a fine layer of sawdust over everything in our garage.

A C grade suggests that customers give businesses the benefit of any doubt, as long as communication continues. This business almost lost the customer due to a slow response, but the customer was still motivated to answer a supplemental list of questions that Angie's List asks, including:

- How much did the final cost compare to the original estimate? *right on*
- How does the value of the work compare to the price? *I got exactly what I paid for*

Law of Symbiosis

- Did you find the company through Angie's List? *no*
- If no, what was the other source? *Recommendation*
- Why did you choose this contractor? *reputation*
- Have you used this company before? *this is the first time I've used this company*
- What did you like most about this contractor? *I thought the salesman was very honest*
- What did you like least about this contractor? *The installation process*
- What surprises came up in the course of the work? *The gap between what the installer planned to do and what we had designed*
- What words of advice would you give other members considering this contractor? *Make sure you understand the details of the proposed design. Ask to see pictures.*
- What words of advice would you give this contractor? *Better quality control on the installation process.*

Note the question about how the customer learned about the company, a personal reference maybe—nice subtle advertising for something like Angie's List. What do you think the effect would be on potential customers if the company had a good response to this complaint?

Angie's List also has a monthly newsletter identifying companies in "the penalty box" for what infraction, for how long, and whether they are doing anything to rectify the problem. Here is an excerpt of one businessperson's attempt to preempt any problems. It is presented as written.

16 IMPORTANT THINGS YOU SHOULD KNOW BEFORE YOU HIRE US: 1.) We charge $50.00 per MAN hour 2.) MONDAY THROUGH FRIDAY we charge a MINIMUM, of $200.00 for our time to come out, which is to cover our gas and time just to come out to you, and it covers up to 4 hours of work. 3.) SATURDAYS We Charge a Minimum of $300.00 for us to come out for any work to be done. ((and you must schedule a Saturday one week in advance. (we all work Monday through Friday, Very long hours, and we like our weekends off and our families need us sometimes as well), so if you can not find time during the week for us to work for you, there is a premium for us to give up our weekend. Also, Saturday work MUST be scheduled at least 1 week in advance, unless it is an Emergency, in which case we charge an additional $100.00 on-top of the $300.00 minimum for Saturday work. (SUNDAYS, are a $400.00 minimum) 4.) I prefer that you Please email your requests for estimates. So I may best assist you, please provide a list of exactly what you need us to do, so that I may send to you the best man for the type of work you need completed. Please provide as much detail as possible and if possible, please provide photos of things that need repair. 5.) PLEASE reserve phone calls for EMERGENCIES only. If you call me I may be in the field or driving between jobs and can not make appointments without viewing my schedule. And the list goes on for another ten points.

This preamble must work because this business has an A rating and received the Angie's List Customer Service Award. Maybe this forthrightness suggests an honest company, something that most customers are hoping to identify up-front. It also lists reasons why it does what it does, making sense of the approach and how the customer saves money.

An organization can no longer count on customer inertia to keep problems at a low key. Problems will find their way onto our interconnected online consciousness and into the hearts and minds of potential customers, and you have to know how to respond. And the response, whether a compliment or a complaint, has to be symbiotic mutualism, a win-win.

Many companies offer a reward to those filling out comment cards, a chance at a thousand dollars or a choice of other prizes. This is hard to do online, as there are so many potential noncompany sites for comments; however, a smart company will seek them out and respond positively to people saying nice things.

More important, however, is to constructively and substantively respond to comments that hurt, accurate or not. Here again is a response to a review as found on Angie's List. The reviewer complained about a poor fitting door and the installer's attitude.

> ...The wall cabinets were measured and ordered by owner. I was told that they would fit. But of course they did not when the fourth cabinet went up i advised the owner of the measurement problem and he authorized me over the phone to trim the cabinet to fit. so I did and installed it. One door was tight to open but it just needed to be adjusted to work. I never said that they did not need to open that cabinet door. LOL

The sink base went in fine but the home owner/plumber installed the shut off lines in the floor and did not secure the pipes to the structure, in lifting the cabinet 18" in the air and coming down the pipes hung up on the cabinet with very little pressure and the unsecured pipe broke off below the floor. This was not standard practice plumbing so the owner had to fix his own mistake or pay me for it. he choose to fix himself.

The amount of trim the owner provided for the crown was not enough so I did the best that could be done with the hard wood stained trim. The seam was off a 32nd of an inch which the owner complained about. I just needed more material to complete.

…and so on for another paragraph.

Symbiosis

Customers are people. Employees are people. Our business partners are people, too. It seems reasonable that if care is taken, a mutualism relationship can be developed. Yet often, a parasitism or prey-predator symbiosis results instead. Good business people understand that complaints can be the royal road to great customer service. A complaint, handled well, increases the chances that customer will become a loyal customer. Mishandled complaints become fuel for prey-predator actions, and poor service or products lead to feelings of parasitism.

Mutualism can be especially difficult to realize with suppliers and distributors. At a base level, it's easy to think of your vendors as parasitic, sucking as much money as they can from you to maximize their profits with little regard for your well-being. Of course, your contractors probably feel the same way as you try to extract as much value from them at the lowest cost.

Depending on your degree of market power relative to your partners, you might be content to flog vendors to squeeze out what you can. For at least some partners, however, you might find greater value in a win-win dynamic. The key to transforming a reciprocally parasitic relationship into a true synergy requires two things: trust and shared incentives.

Trust, of course, must grow over time as each party demonstrates loyalty (or at least absence of disloyalty) to agreed protocols and operates transparently with one another. Trust is enhanced through mutual respect, as well. The Golden Rule applies to how we treat our partners if we value the relationship. Treating vendors dismissively or patronizingly – like "the help" – will lead only to grudges.

Shared incentives start with identifying common goals, and then aligning efforts and setting service level agreements to collectively reach the targets. In some cases, the benefit of shared incentives becomes so great that partners will go out of their way to invest in improving the capabilities of one another.

We have consulted with several large manufacturers that have invested in technology or process improvement advisory services for their partners to make them as productive as possible. In the Lean world, this extreme level of mutualism is referred to as an extended value stream, in which the extent of close collaboration extends beyond the boundaries of the company itself to create a virtual organization.

You must always create a symbiotic relationship with your customers; this is a *we* mentality. Together you will determine needs and provide whatever that is, seek feedback on satisfaction, and ensure that the customer is happy with the results—*every time*. Periodic customer surveys do not create symbiosis. A response of "No problem" when a customer says "Thank you" does not create symbiosis.

Symbiosis is a kind of intimacy, somewhat easy to create in human-to-human contacts, not so easy in the online environment. Seek symbiosis with all customers and employees, no matter what method of contact you use.

Survival Guide

Consider your relationships with your customers and partners.

- Describe examples of *mutualism* in your organization's relationships (we're-in-this-together mentality). What can you do to encourage greater mutualism?
- Describe examples of *parasitism* in your organization's relationships (where compromises become sacrifices). What can your organization do to be less parasitic or to reduce your exposure to the parasitic behavior of others?
- Describe examples of the *prey-predator* dynamic in your organization's relationships (creating winners and losers). What can your organization do to be more constructive in its relationships with others or to be less vulnerable to being the prey?

Law of Information

Where is the life we have lost in living? Where is the wisdom we have lost in knowledge? Where is the knowledge we have lost in information?
-T. S. Eliot

10 | *Information: Precious as Water*

Many of us from developed countries are oblivious to the realities of life: that meat doesn't grow in clear plastic wrap but is hacked out of the bodies of dead animals; that we indeed pave over paradise and put in a parking lot; and although we like our lawns green, that water is a scarce and precious commodity in many places. However, we civilized folks have our own life-is-hard realities, unnatural as they may be.

We sometimes call our current epoch the Information Age. We have computers that can process petabytes of data. Our phones can connect us to people across the planet and store entire libraries-worth of knowledge. One third of the population cannot remember a world without the Internet.

If you can find yourself in one of the few remaining corners of the world without connectivity to some form of communication, you are likely to be overwhelmed with the utter silence of a deep forest absent a constant barrage of electronic notes, messages, advertisements, alerts, and reminders.

Our rapid progress in tools for and approaches toward capturing and processing data permeates all aspects of our daily business. Such advancement has given rise to a broad class of professionals known as knowledge workers. Information management is a competency that can be an important competitive differentiator, especially in industries where fractions of seconds or millions of daily transactions are part of the business.

Why then, in this age of exponential advancements in supercomputing power, does it often feel like we are no smarter and no more capable of understanding our place in the market than organizations did generations ago? The simple answer is that we aren't any smarter. In fact, in many ways, we are even less able to understand our environments and to make decisions than we were decades or even centuries ago.

This seemingly counterintuitive dynamic boils down to a simple but fundamental misunderstanding: few people understand what information is, what it can be, and what it should be. There are few words in the common lexicon that are more often misused than "information."

We find in our consulting work that it's often useful to provide the following basic framework as a starting point when explaining the concept and *context* of information. On the next page is a graphic we often discuss.

States of Knowledge

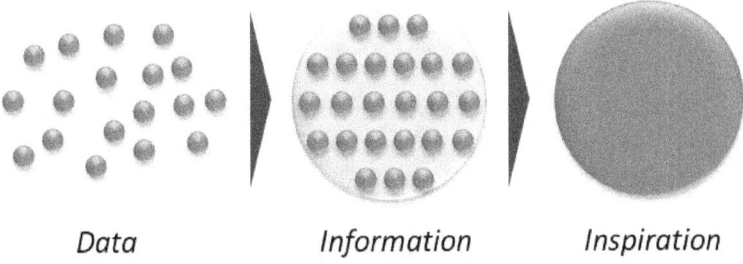

Data *Information* *Inspiration*

It's important to understand that data and information are not the same thing, even though both terms are often used interchangeably. Data are facts or observations. Data alone provide no meaning or understanding, they just *are*. Information, on the other hand, is the assimilation of data in such a way that they provide actionable insight. Information is like water in that we need it to survive; however, also like water, too much information can lead to flooding and drowning.

Beyond information is the ultimate, yet elusive, state of knowledge: inspiration. Inspiration is the impetus to turn understanding into a new, innovative, and plausible concept.

Data

Data collection is the first step in the knowledge progression. Data come in a variety of forms, including electronic, written, symbolic, verbal, and experiential. The ease by which electronic data can be collected means that often the challenge with data collection is less about finding *any* data than about finding *useful* data. Mark Twain observed that when it comes to data there are "lies, damn lies, and statistics." Watch any political debate or read opposing editorials and it is apparent how easily data can be manipulated or just plain made up.

In business, lack of consistent data definitions and lack of clarity about the provenance of facts regularly leads to lack of credibility. One of the easiest ways to dispute an unpopular perspective is to attack the believability of the underlying data. If data are the raw ingredients of information, then they can result in an inauspicious foundation on which to build actionable insight and inspiration.

The norm in business is for managers to rely on data collected from indirect sources instead of direct observation to piece together a mosaic view of the business environment. Customer satisfaction surveys, sales figures, press releases, volumes of financial and operational data, and thick statistical presentations from contracted research are all combined to provide a window to the world.

It's frightening to observe the incredible resources and time spent by consultants and support staff to abstractly represent the world to executives under the light of conference room projectors. The clearest perspective executives could gather would be through simple direct observation. Overreliance on filtered facts to portray the world instead of going into that world to talk with customers, partners, suppliers, and employees directly is like papering over a window with a crude watercolor rendition of the same view.

It is perhaps understandable why we prefer to pore over reams of eight pitch printouts and research decks generated by expensive systems and advisors. It's easier to hide behind our desks than to look our customers, partners, and employees in the eye and to witness firsthand what they have to experience each day due to our decisions or inaction.

Practitioners of the Lean management philosophy advocate "going to gemba" as the primary source of data collection. "Gemba" is roughly translated from Japanese as "the place where value is created." Going to gemba means that leaders should leave the comfortable confines of their offices and conference rooms. Leaders should spend their time in direct observation of the entire value stream, starting with the end customer and working upstream through the value creation process.

John Shook of the Lean Enterprise Institute recommends that this gemba walk should consist of three considerations: go see, ask why, show respect. "Go see" means leaders should observe the interaction of people, process, and technology in the delivery of value and identify where value is—and is not—being created. "Ask why" encourages leaders to work with employees to dig deep into the value stream to uncover root causes of problems that prevent value creation and identify opportunities to generate new efficiencies. "Show respect" reminds leaders to treat those they observe with respect for the work they do and to identify and mitigate indications of mistreatment.

This is not to suggest that only empirical data are useful. To be sure, some facts that can be collected from trusted, calibrated, and well-defined sources can help to augment the data we collect through direct observation. However, like an airplane pilot, we should only accept data provided through our gauges as supporting facts and not allow them to supersede our own direct observation.

Information

The only reason to receive or disseminate information is to decide if an action is needed, and if so, inform what that action should be. Information should motivate the receiver to act when prudence calls for a change.

Facts and figures presented in reports or posted on walls may be interesting, but without context have little intrinsic value. Data don't answer "so what?" Information, data presented in the context of stated targets, for example, helps to answer the "so what?" question. Should I be happy about that number? Should I be encouraged by those customer survey results? Do we need to make changes to improve our situation, and if so, where should we start? This is true in the world of Darwin and in your world too.

To understand the value of information, start at the outcome. What behavior do you want to elicit? The outcome could be a change in attitude to stimulate behavior, new information to promote optimism to increase risk-taking or learning options that could lead to accepting company stock instead of a salary bump. Information could enable departments to work better together. Information should lead to better decision-making. Whatever the use, information is most valuable when the desired outcome is defined so the content, the audience, and the communication and action medium are chosen well. Information is simple. It should be actionable and the absolute minimum needed to be effective.

Inspiration

Information must be actionable; however, if we fail to take action on it, information is like data—much work for little to no benefit. Data can lead to information; information can lead to inspiration. Below are some examples. The first is from Steve Jobs as he and Steve Wozniak tried to get Atari and HP interested in their personal computer.

> So we went to Atari and said, 'We've got this amazing thing, even built with some of your parts and what do you think about funding us? Or we'll give it to you. We just want to do it. Pay our salary, we'll come work for you.' They said 'No'. Then we went to Hewlett-Packard; they said, 'We don't need you. You haven't got through college yet'.

And from Theodore Roosevelt…

> It's not the critic who counts, not the one who points out how the strong man stumbled or how the doer of deeds might have done them better. The credit belongs to the man who is actually in the arena; whose face is marred with the sweat and dust and blood; who strives valiantly; who errs and comes up short again and again; who knows the great enthusiasms, the great devotions and spends himself in a worthy cause and who, at best knows the triumph of high achievement and who at worst, if he fails, at least fails while daring greatly so that his place shall never be with those cold and timid souls who know neither victory nor defeat.

Poems can inspire. This is an excerpt from "If" by Rudyard Kipling:

> If you can dream - and not make dreams your master,
> If you can think - and not make thoughts your aim;

> If you can meet with Triumph and Disaster
> And treat those two impostors just the same;
> If you can bear to hear the truth you've spoken
> Twisted by knaves to make a trap for fools,
> Or watch the things you gave your life to, broken,
> And stoop and build 'em up with worn-out tools.

Even quotes from unknown sources can inspire.

> The stone-age didn't end because they ran out of stones.

> With every willing pair of hands comes a free brain.

> A mistake is only a mistake if you don't learn from it.

Everyone can understand the difference between a slide show with data and information and a heartfelt story told by the chairman of the board or, even better, a customer. Yet our default is the data-filled slide show.

Slides are easier, concrete, expected, and low-risk. An inspirational story is unpredictable, chancy, and maybe even unprofessional. A slide can contain twenty years of data in a single graph. A story may have only one simple theme. A slideshow can include colors, movement, even sounds. A story relies on the skill of the storyteller and the imagination of the audience.

Data are what we collect from our environment. Information is what we glean from the data. Inspiration is how we reconstruct our environment and our role in it. We're reminded of the story of the great hockey player Wayne Gretzky, who said his success was because he did not skate to where the puck was, but to where it would be. That's inspired hockey.

Enough said. This chapter has provided minimal data, some information, and we hope has inspired you to behave differently.

This is the sequence of knowledge:

> Data → Information → Inspiration

Stop in your organization at the point you think is best.

Survival Guide

Consider how well your organization uses knowledge:

- How much effort is put into collecting and reporting data? Do you ever feel it is difficult to make confident decisions due to the sheer volume of facts and figures to consider?
- Is it a common practice to develop information instead of reporting data by accompanying facts and figures with targets and other forms of context? How easy is it to review reports and determine if the data are informing a clear decision-making direction?
- When a decision is made, is it supported by swift and decisive action? Are most decisions accompanied by intrinsically motivated execution, or do people have to be motivated to fight through inertia?

Conclusion: Living Another Day

There is no more fertile jungle than a tropical rain forest. And there is no more fertile tropical rain forest than the Amazon rain forest in Brazil. In just a few acres, six hundred and fifty species of trees can be found. This is more than grow in Canada and the United States combined. With the lush growing conditions, it was long believed that jungles were places where species could find and retain a survival niche that would last a long time; species could coexist by specializing to a particular environment. Not so.

Per the husband and wife team of ecologists, Phyllis Coley and Thomas Kursar, the jungle is a place of intense competition. Rain forest plants, for example, not having to cope with cold or wind as other plants do, harbor many species of insects, all busy devouring leaves, seeds, stems, and bark. Plants must create defenses, and they do, including attracting insects that eat other insects, growing hairs that impede insect movement, and even producing toxins, different ones to poison different species of insects. In turn, insects evolve defenses against these plant armaments. The result is a continuous arms race, one that rewards the plant or insect that best adapts to existing conditions.

A current business equivalent to the Brazilian rain forest is the Internet. Not too long ago, giant start-ups like eBay and Amazon were reliant on Sun servers, Oracle databases, and Cisco networking. Today, new enterprises can jump on Amazon web services, find their niche and grow like a weed. However, low cost and ease of entry is like the rain forest, a welcoming environment that means intense competition.

The price of survival is constant vigilance:

- To customer needs and wants
- Of the value of internal structures and policies
- Of creating a hospitable environment for employees
- To ensure flow of everything, especially inspiration

Survival of the fittest is a simple and compelling reality. Your company is no different than any organism trying to find food and stay alive. The fittest company is the one that can adapt to changing conditions well and quickly, internally and externally. Stay alert to the new laws of evolution, know what keeps you from adapting when you need to so your business can survive, sustain, and succeed.

Notes, Quotes, Do's and Don'ts

If you're going to do something, do the right something.
-Pat Edmonds and Bob Brown

Notes

Introduction

As we thought about the book's theme, survival of the fittest, we wondered how long any business could be expected to survive. How long is long? We were surprised to learn that in one case, long is over a thousand years—and a family business at that. Business is not just about making money; it is about the people doing the work and avoiding zombification. Coffers filled with gold will be lost to an indifferent workforce. Here's just a little of what we learned about Kongō Gumi.

From James Olan Hutcheson, *Businessweek*, on April 16, 2007:

> Kongō Gumi also boasted some internal positives that enabled it to survive for centuries. Its last president, Masakazu Kongō, was the fortieth member of the family to lead the company. He has cited the company's flexibility in selecting leaders as a key factor in its longevity. Specifically, rather than always handing reins to the oldest son, Kongō Gumi chose the son who best exhibited the health, responsibility, and talent for the job. Furthermore, it wasn't always a son. The 38th Kongō to lead the company was Masakazu's grandmother.
>
> Another factor that contributed to Kongō Gumi's extended existence was the practice of sons-in-law

taking the family name when they joined the family firm. This common Japanese practice allowed the company to continue under the same name, even when there were no sons in a given generation.

So if you want your family business to last a long time, the story of Kongō Gumi says you should mingle elements of conservatism and flexibility. Stay in the same business for more than a millennium, but vary from the convention (like the principle of primogeniture) as needed to preserve the company.

We also wondered how much effect an individual can have against the infinite power of evolution. Alice Roberts in her wonderful book, *The Incredible Unlikeliness of Being* (2015, pp. 346-347), gave us permission to be hopeful. She said this about adapting to the environment:

> ...environment also contains other animals from its own species, each of which may be a competitor, an ally, an enemy, or a mate...Our animal must also be a good "fit" in its social context in order to survive and thrive...The environment shapes us, but we're also shaping the environment that shapes us.

What we do today and plan to do tomorrow has a profound effect on the world we live in.

1
Law of Connectedness
Small and Organized Beats
Big and Strong and Smart

Just as in the physical world, where incessant drops of water can wear away mountains, it's the little things in life that can move what seems immovable. Which would you prefer, a handful of Goliaths or a hundred Davids?

For more information on how biological superorganisms are studied to help develop the field of artificial neural networks, see Roberto A. Vazquez and Beatriz A. Garro, "Training Spiking Neural Models Using Artificial Bee Colony",
http://www.ncbi.nlm.nih.gov/pmc/articles/PMC4331474/

Individual humans can also be thought of as superorganisms when we consider that a typical human digestive system contains 10^{13} to 10^{14} microorganisms

http://en.wikipedia.org/wiki/Superorganism

> The simplicity and order of an authoritarian organization make it an almost irresistible temptation. Yet it is counter to the principles of individual freedom and smothers the creative growth of man. Freedom requires orderly restraint. The restraints imposed by the need for cooperation are minimized with a lattice organization. — Bill Gore, Founder of W. L. Gore & Associates

Channel the Wisdom of Crowds

This is a fun and surprising game we have played with our university classes.

1. Fill a large, clear bowl with small candy, like M&M's or Skittles. For simplicity, you can count the pieces in one bag of candy and multiply by the number of bags you use or can extrapolate by weighing each bag.
2. Ask each person in a group (ideally, at least ten people) to record how many pieces they estimate are in the bowl.
3. Once all people have guessed, average the estimates of the group. You are likely to find that the average estimate is closer to the actual number than any individual guess, especially if the group is large.

2
Law of Living Things
Natural Human Tendencies
Can Kill (Your Business)

It almost goes without saying, but not quite: people are your most important asset. Yet most are not engaged. Most are expected to do the work and nothing else. As cogs in a wheel, we really don't want them to change; that would mess up the wheel.

See report on Conference Board's Consumer Research Center's study at CNN Money article, Julianne Pepitone,

"U.S. job satisfaction hits 22-year low" in http://money.cnn.com/2010/01/05/news/economy/job_satisfaction_report/

Read more information about the impact of workplace stress, Rebecca Maxon, Fairleigh Dickinson University, "Stress in the Workplace: A Costly Epidemic" http://www.fdu.edu/newspubs/magazine/99su/stress.html and Helge Hoel, Kate Sparks & Cary L. Cooper, University of Manchester Institute of Science and Technology, "The Cost of Violence/Stress at Work and the Benefits of a Violence/Stress-Free Working Environment," Report Commissioned by the International Labour Organization (ILO) Geneva.

Here are a few more thoughts.

Train people well enough to do the work and train them so they can develop as coworkers too.

Use "we" all the time, and mean it.

Ask yourself: What are we doing to grow the people, and how do we know if it's working?

How does what my company is doing now make sense?

Grow means to become a better worker and a better person—both, not either/or.

Does your company have an employee growth plan?

Stress is one of the major reasons for absenteeism.

Generational categories are ridiculous.

3
Law of Design
Form Must Always Follow Function

We were amazed, when we thought about it and discussed it over coffee many times, how a business automatically becomes a feudal structure. Is your company a strict hierarchy? Why?

While preparing this section we were called by an office products company checking about their service. It so happened we had visited their website the day before to place an order. The interface wasn't simple; we were moved to different pages, some of which no longer contained the product identification number. After three attempts to complete our purchase, we left that site and moved to a competitor's site where we completed our purchase within two minutes. We told the young woman of our experience, for which she apologized as sincerely as a person can. She then said it should have been easy and went on to explain why. We said it didn't matter how easy it was for her, but only for us. She apologized with the same degree of sincerity, which was impressive.

The conversation continued, and she apologized two more times, the last one with a hint of exasperation. Had she not told us it was easy and not apologized so much, she could have won us back. She did ask for us to describe the problem, but made the mistake of trying to minimize it. She should have talked about us, not about the process. She was probably well trained though.

4

Law of Attraction and Neglect
What You Don't See Can
Kill You

No one can deny the sex appeal of the movies' leading men and leading women. But would you like to marry one? Pretty doesn't equate to nice. Nature has produced miniature dramas exemplified by the male black widow spider: attracted to the mate of his dreams only to be devoured after the greatest experience of his life when the female decides the intended mate is food.

5

Law of the Living Dead
Zombie Companies Create Zombie Employees

Reference the following articles about wasted time in meetings, Susan Friedmann, "Business Meetings: A Big Waste of Workplace Time?" PRLog, http://www.prlog.org/12137510-business-meetings-big-waste-of-workplace-time.html and *"To Meet or Not to Meet - What are the Questions?"* Work 911, http://work911.com/planningmaster/planningarticles/tomeetornottomeetwhatrquestions.htm

See *Forbes* article, Steve Cooper, "Make More Money By Making Your Employees Happy" http://www.forbes.com/sites/stevecooper/2012/07/30/make-more-money-by-making-your-employees-happy/

"Dialogue" is not simply conversation. Further your understanding by checking out the Wikipedia explanation.

For more information on the Seven People Assets, please see Robert Brown, *The Dark Matter and Dark Energy of Lean Thinking*, 2014

Zombies really exist in nature: fungi in the genus *Ophiocordyceps* infest an ant's brain, manipulating the ant to drunkenly wander along the rain forest leaves before clamping its jaws around the main vein on the leaf's underside mass grave. The fungus then shoots a stalk out of the zombie ant's head, which fruits fungal spores that consume the ant's corpse.

Norman Bodek notes: "Why is inventory measured and reported down to the penny, but an organization's most important asset, the knowledge and creativity of people, is nowhere on a balance sheet? The underutilization of people is one of Lean's forms of waste, but where is it measured? Human Resources, HR, used to be 'HRD'… Human Resources Development. No longer. What happened to the 'D'? We must bring back the 'D'!"

6
Law of Malignancies
Internal Competition Causes Cancer

As famed quality guru W. Edwards Deming described it, when performance ratings are used, "Everyone propels himself forward, or tries to, for his own good, on his own life preserver. The organization is the loser."

The Myth of the Visionary Leader is described in the *Boston Globe* article, Leon Neyfakh, "Myth of the Visionary Leader," 20 October, 2013.

A 1999 report by Fairleigh Dickinson University reported that one third of people surveyed considered quitting their jobs because of stress and 14 percent actually did. Rebecca Maxon, "Stress in the Workplace: A Costly Epidemic."

The BBC News reported the impact of work-related stress in "Work stress 'increases heart attack risk'" (5 August, 2003)

See Gallup Poll information on workplace stress costs at "The High Cost of Disengaged Employees," http://www.gallup.com/businessjournal/247/the-high-cost-of-disengaged-employees.aspx

The Enron dynamic is described in C. William Thomas, *The Rise and Fall of Enron*, Journal of Accountancy, April 2002, pp. 41-45, 47-48. © 2002 by Texas Society of CPAs.

For more on "heightism," see Jonathan Rauch, "Short Guys Finish Last," *The Economist*, 23 December, 1995 http://www.jonathanrauch.com/jrauch_articles/height_discrimination_short_guys_finish_last/index.html

7
Law of Good Health
Cooperation Cures Cancer

As we consult with various organizations, it is interesting and sad to observe internal competition that decreases the effect of every leader and employee. Maybe the cause goes back to school and the competition for grades. Or maybe it's a current problem and is fueled by yearly performance reviews. Or maybe it's trying to look good in meetings. No matter what the cause, we have seen few companies that can claim true leadership teams. And just as bad, we have seen few managers who teach rather than evaluate.

8
Law of Boundaries
Amoebas Rule

We are impressed by amoebas. What they do, they do well. They are simple creatures doing simple things. We are complex creatures doing complex things. Our suggestion is that we continue to be complex creatures, but begin to do simple things really well. It worked for Coach John Wooden and his UCLA basketball team. Simple has so many advantages. One is you can tell easier if it's working. Another is that people can actually do it.

9
Law of Symbiosis
Survival Makes for Strange Bedfellows

Love and hate are not opposites; love and indifference are opposites. Love and hate are intense feelings that can flip-flop, sometimes in an instant. The idea in this law is to connect with the customer in all the finest ways it is to be human. People are the only reason to be in business; embrace them.

10
Law of Information
Information: Precious as Water

From now on, consider that gathering and processing data is a destructive form of intellectual masturbation and that if you do it too much, you'll go blind.

More Quotes We Like

There are two kinds of people: Those who do the work and those who take the credit. Try to be in the first group because there is less competition there.
-Indira Gandhi

There is nothing noble in being superior to some other person. The true nobility is in being superior to your previous self.
-Indian Proverb

Whenever there is fear, you will get wrong figures.
-W. Edwards Deming

In the long history of humankind (and animal kind, too) those who learned to collaborate and improvise most effectively have prevailed.
-Charles Darwin

Eliminate numerical quotas, including Management by Objectives.
-W. Edwards Deming

There is nothing so useless as doing efficiently that which should not be done at all.
-Peter F. Drucker

We are too busy mopping the floor to turn off the faucet.
-Author Unknown

The man who will use his skill and constructive imagination to see how much he can give for a dollar, instead of how little he can give for a dollar, is bound to succeed.
-Henry Ford

He who rejects change is the architect of decay. The only human institution which rejects progress is the cemetery.
-Harold Wilson

Failure to change is a vice.
-Hiroshi Okuda

You can't stay in your corner of the Forest waiting for others to come to you. You have to go to them sometimes.
-Winnie the Pooh

Don't water your weeds.
-Harvey MacKay

Do's and Don'ts

Feed the owners regularly, but don't allow them to become fat and lazy.

Don't store useless information.

Don't put up walls.

Treat employees as if they were real people.

Don't do annual performance evaluations. If you're growing people and not zombies, you won't need them.

Don't create waste.

Connect with employees as if you were a real person.

Don't lie.

Don't stay silent

Know what is rewarding to your employees and provide that.

Don't conduct needless meetings or meetings that take one minute more than necessary.

Make sure your business is in the business of providing value to customers and not self-preservation.

Don't isolate anyone.

Create an inspiring vision for your company.

Don't transmit filtered information.

Take the long view.

Don't work on weaknesses where others are strong.

Don't lay off anyone except as the last resort.

Work closely and collaboratively with your suppliers.

Improvement should be the only constant (along with operating from a universal set of values).

Plan for the eventual death of your company.

Let people know you will always tell the truth, but you will not be able to always tell them everything.

Don't put process before people.

About the Authors

Pat Edmonds is an experienced management consultant and university professor, a niche that allows him to act out his ongoing passion for helping organizations to be better by fostering better environments for their employees to thrive. He graduated from the United States Naval Academy, has an MBA from Stanford, and is a certified Lean Six Sigma Master Black Belt. He was a Navy pilot when he was young, but now he just flies in the back of commercial airplanes.

Pat lives in the Seattle area with his wife, children, and greyhounds.

Bob Brown, the president of Collective Wisdom, Inc., has been a performance enhancement consultant for over forty years. He primarily conducts one- and two-day workshops on "Mistake-Proofing Teams," "The HST Change Model," and "The People Side of Lean Thinking," which cover creating high-performing teams, communicating, problem solving, organizational development and improving people interactions with Lean tools. He is also a popular keynote speaker. He has a doctorate in psychology and is a certified Lean leader.

Bob lives with his wife and various animals north of Seattle.

His website is www.collwisdom.com.

www.ingramcontent.com/pod-product-compliance
Lightning Source LLC
Chambersburg PA
CBHW051639170526
45167CB00001B/260